SALVAGE, REDIRECTION, OR CUSTODY?

Remedial Education in the Community Junior College

By John E. Roueche

ERIC Clearinghouse for Junior College Information
American Association of Junior Colleges
Monograph Series

ERIC CLEARINGHOUSE FOR JUNIOR COLLEGE INFORMATION

The Educational Resources Information Center (ERIC) was organized in 1965 by the United States Office of Education. It has as its prime responsibility the acquisition, analysis, and dissemination of information relevant to American education. In the three years of its existence, it has become a valuable source of data and ideas.

ERIC operates through a central office in the United States Office of Education, a Document Reproduction Service, and a network of specialized clearinghouses. Each of the clearinghouses is responsible for bringing under bibliographic control the literature of a segment of the education field. In addition, it analyzes, collates, and disseminates information through publications and other media.

The ERIC Clearinghouse for Junior College Information operates under contract with the United States Department of Health, Education and Welfare, Office of Education, as a joint project of the University of California, Los Angeles, Graduate School of Education and the University Library. Arthur M. Cohen, assistant professor of higher education is principal investigator and director of the project; Lorraine Mathies, head of the Education-Psychology Library is coinvestigator; and John E. Roueche is associate director.

The Clearinghouse was established in June 1966. Since that time it has collected, indexed, and abstracted documents containing information relative to all phases of junior college operations—students, staff, plant, curriculums, and organization. Its particular acquisitions emphasis has been on research studies produced by junior colleges and on publications reporting results of research concerning junior colleges.

Information dissemination activities take a variety of forms. The Clearinghouse sends abstracts of documents into the ERIC system where they appear in *Research in Education*, a United States Office of Education monthly publication. It also prepares bibliographies and other types of specialized materials for distribution to the field. One of the Clearinghouse's most popular publications is *Junior College Research Review*, a monthly report of research findings and recommendations compiled by the Clearinghouse staff and published by the American Association of Junior Colleges.

With this monograph, the Clearinghouse introduces a new series of information analysis activities. There are many topics of concern to junior college educators that warrant study in depth. Several times each year the Clearinghouse staff will review the problems in one such area, consider the research literature relative to that topic, and prepare a report. Remedial education in the community junior college is the first topic to be accorded that treatment. Future monographs will consider personality assessments of college teachers, instructional processes in the junior college, the state of the art of junior college research, and similar matters of concern.

This monograph is being published by American Association of Junior Colleges. The Association has been generous in its support of the Clearinghouse's effort to disseminate information. Our special thanks to members of the Association and to the United States Office of Education for making possible the production of this report and other Clearinghouse publications.

Arthur M. Cohen

CONTENTS

FOREWORD

"Salvage, redirection, custody" are three charged words that characterize not only the disadvantaged, low-aptitude students but also the entire concept of the open-door policy of admission in the community junior colleges. In this study, John Roueche focuses our attention on a special aspect, a natural concomitant of the open-door policy, namely, on how effectively the junior colleges are educating the disadvantaged, low-aptitude students.

In a previous report of the Clearinghouse for Junior College Information, John Roueche performed a valuable service to junior college educators by providing an annotated listing of the projects in this field. In *Salvage, Redirection, or Custody?* he does more than report—he interprets, he makes critical judgments, he indicates the direction of efforts, and he suggests other avenues of exploration. Moreover, in the first comprehensive report on this function of the junior college he raises issues, ventures hypotheses, pinpoints successes, and not surprisingly becomes involved in semantics. Dr. Roueche's analysis of the multiple facets of the subject is kaleidoscopic. About the time we think we have distinguished a color, another appears redirecting our attention. Perhaps this is inevitable; it must remain so until a dominant color appears upon which to fix our attention. But how does one do this in a kaleidoscopic situation without stroboscopic power?

In his chapter on "The Implications," the author comes close to accomplishing this feat. He writes, "Perhaps the junior colleges must now determine what students are going to learn in remedial programs, the conditions of learning, and how this learning can be evaluated."

To this could be added another point: the colleges must determine which of the students are capable of learning.

We are indebted to John Roueche for making it plain that the education of this group is a national problem, not only for the junior colleges but for all segments of education. Unless solutions are found, it will become as serious for junior colleges as it is now for the elementary and secondary schools. And, as in the latter, the problem has political and social implications as well. To mention the obvious, the programs today lead to *de facto* segregation.

As junior college education becomes universal, the political and social implications will intrude more insistently into the educational problems, especially in our inner cities. Because of the community concern with education, the urgency for finding solutions to the problems relating to the education of the disadvantaged, low-aptitude students has increased. Were the students white, a good deal less urgency might be involved, a greater frankness might be expressed, and more realistic approaches might be undertaken.

Dr. Roueche makes it plain that the effort to modify the regular programs has not been successful. It would have been startling if he had discovered a radical departure from the traditional educational patterns. We may also add that the lack of success could have been predicted, since the students had already failed in high school programs that are not much different from those in the colleges. But now that this study reveals the inadequacies of most of the present programs, we should expect college educators to seek radically different patterns of education.

In his chapter on "The Programs," the author refers to some revolutionary approaches, indicating that some colleges are departing from traditional practices.

In conclusion, a warning should be voiced. Observers often are more pessimistic about the efficacy of the programs than are the participants, probably because the participants are doing something, see results that the observers are unable to see, look forward to a solution or solutions that may be as unexpected and as far-reaching as some of the discoveries made by scientists. Not all discoveries flow from hypotheses or designs. Some do come from intuition. This could be construed as pollyannaism, romanticism, if it were not that successes, minor though they may be, are reported.

Yet, we must agree with John Roueche that in this area the junior college is on trial. For years it has boasted of its goal to "strive to offer what the people can profit by." Now it has the opportunity to make good on this claim. John Roueche in the first and second chapters reminds us of these statements regarding "The Open Door" and "Educational Opportunity for All." For some, they may be embarrassing reminders of unfulfilled promises. For most, they will be pricks of conscience that will act as prods to greater effort in transforming these ideals into realities.

John Lombardi
Assistant Superintendent
Los Angeles City School Districts

INTRODUCTION

The open-door policy of the community junior college implies acceptance of the concept of universal higher education. In accepting this ideal, the community college thus becomes committed to provide an education for all high school graduates and others who can profit from instruction. This concept further necessitates an expanded curriculum to match the expanded base of scholastic aptitude among the students who enter the open door. Instead of four or five objectives, the students bring hundreds. Instead of a minority of "poor" students, junior colleges find that group in a majority. Instead of a relatively homogeneous group from a dominant stratum of society, there is now a heterogeneous group—a cross section of the total population (84).*

One of the most pressing problems in the community junior college today centers around the student who, for various reasons, is assigned to one or more remedial courses. This report represents an effort to assemble and collate pertinent research related to remedial students in community colleges, programs that are presently available to them, and the success of these programs in providing educational opportunities for these students.

There is much controversy, confusion, and disagreement over the terms that are applied to remedial students. In that community junior colleges use a variety of aptitude and achievement tests, there is little agreement as to whether remedial students exemplify "low ability" or "low achievement." Other terms in use add greatly to the confusion. Whether or not one agrees with the euphemisms is really not of importance—community junior colleges usually provide the same educational programs for all students in the designated category

* Bracketed numbers refer to bibliographical entries, pages 58-67.

regardless of the distinctions made. This practice indicates that the typical community junior college does not bifurcate its program so that the students designated "low ability" and "low achieving" may be accommodated. In this report, the terms "low achiever" and "remedial" are used interchangeably to define a student who either scored below a given percentile on the institution's placement examinations or who did not achieve a C average in high school. This is the student who, for a variety of reasons, is assigned to a remedial course.

Likewise, the labels assigned to the programs for these students vary widely from institution to institution. The terms "remedial" and "developmental" are often used interchangeably. There is, however, a subtle difference. "Remedial" implies the remediation of student deficiencies in order that the student might enter a program for which he was previously ineligible. While many institutions refer to their remedial endeavors as "developmental," the term actually has a different connotation. Developmental refers to the development of skills or attitudes and may or may not have anything to do with making a student eligible for another program.

Research on developmental programs, as defined above, is virtually nonexistent. The programs are too recent in origin for a body of research to be available. There is a paucity of evidence on the efforts at remediation even though the most frequently offered course in the typical community college is remedial English. Therefore, this report is limited to research on *remedial* programs, their objectives, and the students and teachers involved in these programs.

No national figures are available that reflect the millions-of-dollars effort at remediation by the nation's community colleges. Perhaps more important, there is little research to indicate whether or not such an effort is successful. This report will present the evidence as it currently exists.

The author wishes to express sincere appreciation to the staff of the Clearinghouse for their assistance and cooperation in completing this study. For advice and assistance in various phases of the writing, thanks are extended to Arthur M. Cohen, B. Lamar Johnson, and M. Stephen Sheldon. Special gratitude is extended to Richard Davis Howe and John R. Boggs for their valuable research assistance in preparing this report.

John E. Roueche

THE OPEN DOOR?

chapter 1 The community junior college is an "open-door" institution. Various leaders in the field have stated the basic concept of admissions as follows:

Some colleges will set certain selective standards for admission and retention of students, but community colleges will keep their doors open to any person, youth or adult, who can profit by what the colleges can offer, and the colleges will strive to offer what the people can profit by (13:482).

The basic criterion for admission to a community junior college is graduation from high school. Individuals eighteen years of age and over who appear capable of profiting from the instruction offered are also eligible for admission in most institutions. By law this admissions policy has been assigned to the community college, which in most states must admit all high school graduates and adults who seek admission.

In recent years, with admissions practices in most four-year colleges becoming more stringent and selective, the "open-door" admissions policy has brought great popularity and support to the community junior college. This policy has been consistent with the democratic concepts of individual worth and educational opportunity for all people (84).

While the community junior college has contributed to the extension of educational opportunity through its concept of the open door and its resulting diverse curricular offerings, there are problems. In a sense, the community junior college has been caught in the middle of the drive to increase the educational level of the nation's population. The four-year college and the university are ill equipped

1

to cope with the increasing numbers of individuals seeking higher education, especially when so many of these students lack even the most rudimentary requirements for the successful completion of most baccalaureate programs. Proponents of the open-door concept have insisted that the community college, with its willingness to offer courses below the collegiate level, has been the salvation of the low achiever (11:268).

Critics of the open door, however, have expressed concern over what actually happens to the low-achieving student. Attrition rates in community junior colleges are alarming. Research findings indicate that as many as 75 per cent of low-achieving students withdraw from college the first year (124:141). Yet, it has been maintained that to admit high school graduates without regard to the quality or depth of their preparation is bound to lead to higher attrition rates—the open door may be simply a license to fail (104:241). It is precisely this problem that has led critics to refer cynically to the open door as a "revolving door." The attrition rate may well be one of the most pressing problems of the community junior college.

Are students in actuality duped or "conned" into entering the community college? Are they led to believe that all previous failures are forgiven and that all will be well if they enter the junior college? One critic characterizes the problems of the open door with the following satire: "Come to us and adjust to life. Bloom early or bloom late. Or drop out without blooming if you must. But do walk through our open door and expose yourself to higher education" (6:203). Perhaps the open-door policy of admissions produces nothing more than an unselected heterogeneous group of people who must determine for themselves what they want to get from the institution (127:33-38). Perhaps there are other reasons.

Community junior colleges have established courses and curricular programs to deal with the low-achieving student. Typically these programs are called "remedial" or "developmental," or one of a score of less common terms. Most of these programs have as their central purpose the remediation of students to the point that they can enter regular college credit courses. Junior colleges, however, report little research regarding the success or failure of students who are forced to enroll in these programs (124:86). With little or no encouragement to investigate this problem, community junior colleges have tended to carry on in a trial-and-error fashion, merely hoping to find some answer. An administrator of a community college recently referred to this kind of educational planning as "flying by the seat of your pants" (19). Courses and programs have been established because another college has a similar program or because there are outside funds to support a particular activity.

Further, it is obvious that, as the four-year institutions and universities raise entrance standards and tend to assume less and less responsibility for remedial programs, the community junior colleges, with their open-door policies, are going to be forced to assume more and more responsibility. The majority of students who formerly populated remedial courses in the four-year institutions are now sitting in community college classrooms (15:1).

The open-door concept is valid only if students are able to succeed in their educational endeavors. Currently, the only tenable value seems to be that enrollment allows a student to say, years after his short tenure, "I went to college." But except for this inestimable benefit, little else is apparent. And, until something is done to determine proper guidelines for teaching low-achieving students, much will continue to be left to chance.

The large majority of students who enroll in remedial courses fail to complete those courses satisfactorily and are doomed to failure or forced to terminate their education. In one typical California public junior college, of the 80 per cent of the entering students who enrolled in remedial English, only 20 per cent of that number continued on into regular college English classes (15:1). If community colleges realize that on the day a low-achieving student walks in the door he is going to fail, the concept of the open door is "in real trouble" (96).

This report will attempt to collate pertinent research findings to answer some of the questions that abound regarding the open door, low-achieving students, and programs needed to afford educational opportunity to all. How did community colleges acquire an open-door admissions policy? Was it a logical extension of the idea of providing educational opportunity for all? Or did community colleges win acceptance by attempting to be all things to all people?

Who are the low-achieving students? What criteria are used to place students in remedial or developmental programs—high school grades? Test scores? What are the characteristics common to these low-achieving students?

Who are the teachers assigned to these programs? Are the instructors in sympathy with the objectives of these programs and with the students? What background and experience have these teachers had to prepare them for teaching remedial students?

What are the programs offered? In what subject areas are remedial programs found? What are the functions or objectives of these programs with respect to the low-achieving student? Are they to salvage? Provide a second chance? Cool him out? Provide a custodial function? Implement a filling station concept?

What research is available that evaluates the successes of programs for the low-achieving community college student? What typically happens to the low achiever in the community junior college? How do students qualify to enter regular college credit courses? Test scores as compared with pretest scores or grades in the remedial course? Can low-achieving students who will succeed or complete a degree program be identified? If so, how?

What are the implications of this research for the community college programs? Should the basic purpose of these programs be changed? Do the findings of the research have implications for instructional processes and media? Should community colleges abandon the public relations approach and base educational decisions on the findings of research? Should junior colleges accept responsibility for student learning?

EDUCATIONAL OPPORTUNITY FOR ALL: THE BACKGROUND

chapter 2

For the past two decades, critics of the community junior college have argued that public two-year institutions were diluting their endeavors by attempting to be all things to all people. Indeed, leading spokesmen for the community college movement have focused attention on the lack of a public image for community junior colleges (91:27). Spokesmen for academe have long insisted that the concept of the open door resulted in the lowering of educational quality in the two-year college. Some leading subject matter specialists frankly insist that the community junior college abolish all courses that are labeled remedial or developmental (100:32).

In response to such critics, it must be stated that community colleges reflect the needs of the society that supports them. It has long been axiomatic in our society that control resides where support originates. Community colleges are established by society to perform certain functions. The open-door policy, so distinctive of the community junior college, evolved as the result of a great national experiment in public education—one that provided for the continued extension of educational opportunities for all people.

The benefits of this experiment are found in every realm of American life—the high standards of living, the great advancements in science and technology, the strength of established democratic institutions, the concern with human rights, and the civic competence of the American people support the basic commitments to education as the backbone of the nation's economic, social, and cultural welfare. The following paragraphs briefly trace the development of this experiment in American education.

Higher education was the last area of educational endeavor to be affected by the efforts to extend and broaden educational opportunities. Historically, higher education in the United States was the privilege of the few rather than the opportunity of the majority. In the early 1800's, the classical college, with its limited curriculum, was the only institution of higher education in existence. The classical college was established and structured primarily to preserve and transmit culture and tradition.

During the nineteenth century, however, social forces developed throughout the nation that eventually resulted in the establishment of new types of collegiate institutions. The free school movement began with the conviction that education was a responsibility of the state. Educational opportunity was broadened to include women. The lyceum movement began and became the forerunner of college extension services of today. Industry developed and with it came a demand for trained personnel and technicians. By 1850, existing American institutions of higher learning were inadequate to meet the manpower needs of a rapidly expanding nation. Oriented to classical learning, capable of educating far fewer students than this nation required, inspired by limited objectives, the existing institutions had to be supplemented not only by additional colleges, but by different types of institutions.

Along with the demand for a broader curriculum and for some choice of subject matter by the student, came an impetus for business, technical, and agricultural courses. Education had become a matter of national necessity. Society was demanding courses and programs beyond the scope of existing institutions. The passage of the Morrill Land Grant Act in 1862 was another step in the extension of educational opportunities to all people. These land grant colleges developed and contributed numerous ideas and techniques to the American education system. They developed the laboratory as their teaching tool; extension services; a concern for the practical, everyday problems of people, which became the basis for much of their research activity; and underlying all of this experimentation was the conviction that higher education was the right of any person who could profit from it. Concomitant with this concept was the belief that colleges existed to serve the American people.

The community junior college is the most recently established institution of postsecondary education. Beginning in the late 1800's and expanding in numbers soon after the turn of the century, the community college has been described as the only educational institution that can truly be called an American social invention (56:3).

The establishment of community junior colleges has been regarded by many as the most obvious effort toward democratizing higher education in the United States. Community junior colleges stress that institutional goals are closely related to the concept that each individual should have the opportunity to progress as far as his interests and abilities will permit. While this concept does not imply that everyone should have the same education, it does demand diversified educational programs, such as those the community junior college strives to make available through its curricular offerings.

Several philosophical assumptions have been basic to the extension of educational opportunities in the United States. Educational programs emerge from the basic philosophy of the nation which they serve. Three assumptions are offered in support of the broad and comprehensive educational system that fostered the development of community junior colleges:

1. Education is necessary for the maintenance of a democracy.

Thomas Jefferson, who assisted in the early formulation of American ideals and goals, expressed this admonition in his writings: "If the nation expects to be ignorant and free, in a state of civilization, it expects what never was and never will be" (75). Continued faith in this ideal of an educated citizenry that can influence its destiny in a democratic manner has been a motivating factor in the American development of public education. The concept that a democratic society cannot exist without a well-educated citizenry is well established. The worldwide political responsibilities of this nation, with its technological economy, its lofty concepts of social as well as political democracy—all of these emphasize the need for more and more education for more and more Americans.

2. Education is essential for the improvement of society.

There is evidence everywhere to prove the value of education in the improvement of society. Education has been most successful in resolving some of the nation's most serious social problems. The Americanization of the large groups of immigrants in the 1890's and early 1900's is one of the most conspicuous success stories in public education. As the exploitation of children and women laborers was brought under control, the schools became the major agencies in replacing the mills, the mines, and the factories as the custodians of the large numbers of displaced Americans (84). Retraining for national manpower needs is one of the major functions of education today. Education is truly a national necessity.

3. Education helps to equalize opportunity for all people.

Throughout our history, the societal purposes of education have been paralleled by individual purposes. This nation was founded on the concept of individual worth. The ideal of democracy is to permit each individual to be educated to the level of his highest potential. It is part of the American dream that young people should have the opportunity to go as far in education as their talents and motivation will permit. Thornton emphasizes the individual purpose of education: The American people were learning what the people of older cultures have learned, that the schools are the social elevators in a hardening social structure (137:33). Variety in education and the ideal of educating everyone to the level of his highest potential are consistent with the American demand for excellence in education.

Education has been and will continue to be the vehicle for personal and social advancement.

In its plan for the establishment of community junior colleges, the State of Florida envisioned community colleges as the most likely agents to extend the opportunity for postsecondary education. One major function of the new community college system in Florida was to remove the identifiable barriers that had prevented two-thirds of the total numbers of young people in Florida from seeking higher education. Those barriers, not confined to Florida, are geography, finances, and motivation (45:12-16).

GEOGRAPHY   Geography is a major factor in determining whether a person will or will not attend post-high school institutions. An examination of the location of homes of students who attend college indicates that in most colleges the student body is rather localized. Even universities that serve an international constituency (such as Harvard or the University of California) typically have a localized student body. Most of Harvard's enrollment comes from the New England area. A sizeable majority of the students attending the University of California live within that state. National studies of the community college indicate that enrollment begins to decline when potential students reside more than fifteen miles from campus and becomes practically nonexistent after thirty-five miles (45:12).

There is conclusive evidence that the percentage of high school graduates who continue their education is much larger in communities where a junior college is located than in those where one is not (7:327-329). In Marianna, Florida, before Chipola Junior College was established, about 8 per cent of the high school graduates went on to colleges and universities. After the community college was established, it was found that the 8 per cent still went away to colleges and universities outside the immediate area. However, an additional 40 per cent of the high school graduates in the area were attending the local community junior college (5:29-31). In a statewide study, 48 per cent of the students enrolled in Florida's community colleges reported that they attended a particular community college because of its proximity to their homes (46:1).

The President's Commission on National Goals (112:7) stated that two-year colleges should be constructed within commuting distance of most high school graduates. Much has already been done to move toward the achievement of this purpose. State surveys of higher education in all sections of the country are recommending plans under which the community junior colleges will "cover" the respective states. Massachusetts and Florida have developed plans under which community colleges will be located within commuting distance of from 95 to 99 per cent of each state's population by 1970. California now has community junior colleges within such distance of 85 to 90 per cent of its population (5:12).

FINANCES Until the advent of the community junior college, college attendance was more dependent upon family income than upon student aptitude. In their report of tuition and fee charges in public junior colleges, D'Amico and Bokelman concluded that "the public junior college has provided opportunity to many people who otherwise would not have continued with education beyond the high school" (34:36-39). The reduced cost factor is an important consideration in students' attendance at a local community college. The reason most often given by students for attending the junior college is lack of financial resources (35:475). Twenty-seven per cent of the students in Florida reported "cost" to be a major factor in their decisions to enroll in a community junior college (46:1).

Most states have taken student costs into account in their long-range master plans. Almost all states have made concerted efforts to keep student costs to a minimum. A policy statement on tuition and fees from Michigan is typical of the state view toward costs in community colleges.

Policies directing the admission of students cannot be viewed without considering the economic implications of collegiate level study. If, for instance, the purposes of the institution include providing post-high school educational opportunities for the youth of the community, it is apparent that substantial tuition and fee charges would impede the implementation of the purpose. Many young people would be screened out on economic grounds. It is not enough to develop a tuition and fee schedule policy in line with the financial needs of the institution. It is necessary to relate this policy to the established purposes of the college, and then provide the necessary financial resources from other sources. This is especially true if the local institution's purposes parallel those generally agreed upon. If they do, tuition and fee charges should be either modest or non-existent. In fact, many believe that the only position which is consistent with the function of the community college as defined in these pages is that there should be no tuition or fees. Such a position represents a goal worth serious consideration by communities interested in the community college (97:24-25).

One reason that community colleges have been established by states is to eliminate the financial barriers to higher education.

MOTIVATION Motivation has been a third barrier to postsecondary education. Many young people have not continued beyond high school because they have not seen the advantages of higher education. This lack of motivation has been partially attributed to the lack of familiarity with the advantages of college education and with the kind of training typically available (137:10). Havighurst and Rodgers characterize the problem of superior students who do not continue their education as a motivational one.

9

Practically all of the superior youths who do not continue their education beyond high school are children of people who have less than a high school education. These families participate in a culture which has little personal contact with higher education. They value a job and an earning career highly for their young people. While these people have come to look favorably on a high school education for their children, they do not regard college as really within the reach of their aspirations or their financial means (66:162).

Even with a burgeoning population, national needs for trained manpower will not permit the waste of human talent that results from lack of motivation. States have established community junior colleges to provide curricular programs that are not typically found in four-year colleges and universities. These programs appeal to students with a broad range of abilities and interests. It has been demonstrated that a variety of programs available to students in proximity to campus helps eliminate the motivation barrier.

The community college has removed barriers to higher education because it is located within commuting distance of the students it serves, has little or no tuition, and is geared to the educational needs of the community in which it is located.

MULTIPURPOSE INSTITUTIONS

Community junior colleges are established to be multipurpose institutions. The purposes are reflective of the needs of the communities in which the colleges are located. In this century, as enrollments and numbers of community colleges have increased, a well-defined set of educational responsibilities ascribed to the community college has evolved.

For instance, after examining 343 periodical articles and finding 1,411 statements of purpose, Campbell assigned the thirty different purposes that he grouped together into four major categories. They were: (1) preparatory (college parallel); (2) terminal and occupational; (3) democratizing higher education; and (4) popularizing higher education (18:30).

The President's Commission on Higher Education studied the purposes of the community college and proposed reduced attention to the transfer or preparatory function and more to the occupational function. Commission concern was for more emphasis upon education for the technician and semiprofessional worker. Specifically, the commission recommended: (1) training for the semiprofessions and occupations requiring no more than two years of post-high school work; (2) general education for students terminating their formal education at the end of two years; (3) adult education; and (4) college parallel work for those students who wish to transfer (111:68-69).

After considering the characteristics of society and the needs of individuals, the Yearbook Committee of the National Society for the Study of Education concluded that the major purposes of community colleges were: (1) preparation for advanced study; (2) vocational education; (3) general education; and (4) community service (including adult education as one of the various services) (102:69). The committee also recognized several unique functions, among them (1) guidance and counseling as a specialized service, and (2) providing low-cost post-high school education in proximity to the homes of students (102:73).

After examining statements of function, Hillway summarized them as (1) democratization of higher education through the extension of greater opportunity to all youth; (2) community services; (3) vocational training for the semiprofessions; (4) more effective adult education; and (5) guidance and rehabilitation (69:83).

A comprehensive statement of purpose has been offered by Edmund J. Gleazer, Jr.: "It is the purpose of the community college to make readily available programs of education beyond the high school which match a wide spectrum of community needs and which relate economically and efficiently to the total pattern of educational opportunity in the area" (139:2).

These statements of purpose reflect the needs of the society that established community junior colleges. In an age of burgeoning enrollments and increasingly selective admissions at the senior colleges and universities, it appears that the open door is a matter of national necessity and concern. For example, under the Master Plan for Higher Education in California, enrollment at the university is now limited to those in the upper one-eighth of high school graduates and at the state colleges, to the upper one-third. In fact, the open door of the community college is now the only avenue of public higher education for two-thirds of the high school graduates in California (5:9).

That society has delegated certain tasks to the community junior college is obvious. What is not so obvious is how well the two-year college has performed these tasks. Research on the community junior college has increased recently. In the period 1918-1963, 608 dissertations were reported that had relevance to the junior college (105). A recent compilation (119) includes 214 titles completed within a three-year period, 1964-1966. Increasingly, the junior college is becoming the subject of intensive research at the graduate level. Research in the community junior college, however, has been almost nonexistent. A recent investigation of institutional research in the junior colleges of the United States found that fewer than 20 per cent of these institutions had formally organized programs of institutional research and fewer than one-third of the colleges surveyed had plans for evaluating their research programs (135). There is especially a paucity of research on programs for the low-achieving students who enter the open door. A collation of research findings indicates that certain patterns are present. These findings are discussed in the remainder of this report.

11

THE
STUDENTS

chapter 3 The composition of the community junior college student body has changed drastically in the last twenty years. Formerly the students were a selected group resolved to finish collegiate preparation for well-defined purposes. Today, by contrast, community junior college students are much more representative of the total population—mentally, socially, and economically (44:58). More and more students are entering the open door—students who are unable to begin college credit courses. They are students with deficiencies that must be remedied.

Students with academic deficiencies enter the community junior college for a variety of reasons. Some do not decide on college early enough in high school to meet selective admissions requirements. Others become motivated too late. Some students have such low academic potential that there is little chance that they can succeed in regular college courses.

Low-achieving students in the community junior college may be identified as those students who suffer from one or more of the following characteristics:

1. Graduated from high school with a low C average or below

2. Are severely deficient in basic skills, i.e., language and mathematics

3. Have poor habits of study (and probably a poor place to study at home)

4. Are weakly motivated, lacking home encouragement to continue in school

5. Have unrealistic and ill-defined goals

6. Represent homes with minimal cultural advantages and minimum standards of living

7. Are the first of their family to attend college, hence have a minimum understanding of what college requires or what opportunities it offers (94:61).

The problem of the remedial student becomes acute when reports of actual numbers of students are examined. A state survey reported that of the 270,000 freshmen who entered California's public junior colleges in 1965, almost 70 per cent (190,000) failed the qualifying examination for English 1A (or the equivalent transfer course) (15:2). Of the 60,500 students enrolled in California public junior college mathematics classes in the fall of 1964, three out of four students were taking courses offered in the high school (17:8).

Even more alarming is the failure rate reported for students who are required to enroll in remedial or developmental courses. A recent investigation found that from 40 to 60 per cent of the students enrolled in remedial English classes in California public junior colleges earned a grade of D or F. Only 20 per cent of the students enrolled in these remedial courses later enrolled in college credit courses (15:61). A high attrition rate can likewise be found in other curricular areas (81:38-44).

How are these students identified and on what bases are they assigned to remedial courses? A recent investigation of remedial programs reported that test scores are used in identifying low-achieving students in 95 per cent of the colleges surveyed. One-third (34 per cent) of the community colleges reported that they used the School and College Ability Test (SCAT) to identify students for placement purposes. The American Council on Education Test (ACE) is used by 21 per cent and the American College Test (ACT) by 18 per cent of the colleges. Other community junior colleges use a variety of tests, including the Scholastic Aptitude Test (SAT), the College Qualification Test (CQT), and various state administered placement tests (Florida, New York, and Washington) (124:34-37).

Low-achieving students are typically identified as scoring below a given percentile on one of these standardized tests. The percentile most frequently used is in the eleventh to fifteenth range (124:37). In addition to standardized test scores, many institutions use high school grades to identify low-achieving students. These are typically reported as grade point averages and/or rank in graduating class. Most colleges use a C average as one criterion in identifying students eligible for regular college credit courses. Students ranking in the lower half of their high school graduating classes, therefore, are those most often identified as low achievers (124:37). For the purpose of this report, low-achieving students will be defined as those who, for whatever reasons, are assigned to remedial or developmental courses in the community junior college.

Students assigned to remedial courses either believe or hope that they will eliminate deficiencies and that eventually they can pursue their intended educational program. Research on these students leads

13

to the conclusion that either remedial students have unrealistic educational goals or that the programs in the community junior colleges are failing to remedy their educational deficiencies. A recent statewide study of students enrolled in remedial English courses in California public junior colleges found that 74 per cent of these students planned to transfer to a four-year college or university while only 23 per cent did not plan to transfer (15:23). When students in California remedial English classes were queried about vocational goals and aspirations, 30 per cent indicated a preference for clerical work and 10 per cent planned to enter a technical field. Thirty per cent of the students indicated that they had no vocational plans (15:23). Of these students in remedial English, the overwhelming majority (89.3 per cent) were employed while attending college. Yet most of these students (75 per cent) did not believe that working had in any way interfered with their college endeavors (15:23).

The subjects of the California study believed that the open door would provide the means for them to achieve their educational objectives. They had enrolled in courses designed to make them eligible for college credit English courses. Yet, from 40 to 60 per cent of these students received a grade of D or F in their remedial English course (15:61).

Other research reports provide a more realistic appraisal of the characteristics of low-achieving students. In a Cooperative Research Monograph (31:16), significant characteristics of remedial students in general mathematics courses were identified as:

1. A dislike for and lack of confidence in handling mathematics

2. An approach to testing characterized by nonflexible organization

3. Emotional disturbances associated with awareness of personal inadequacy

4. Lack of self-confidence in relations with instructors

5. A prevalent prediction of unfavorable outcomes for self and peers in school situations.

A negative correlation between student motivation and grades earned in remedial mathematics was also reported (31:16). These research studies indicate a real gap between remedial student aspirations and student success.

An institutional problem is the question of what to call these students. Probationary students are referred to by a score of terms and almost no one agrees on the precise meaning of any of them. "Low achiever" is widely used when referring to students enrolled in remedial programs (145:17). "Low ability" is also a common term (125:22-28). Other words used to identify these students are "marginal," "probationary," "special," "prematriculant," and "developmental." "Disadvantaged" and "underprivileged" are recent additions to the plethora of terms in the field. While these terms convey quite different meanings to their users, more often than not they are used interchangeably. A national investigation found that about half (47 per cent) of the community junior colleges admit low-achieving students as "regular" students so as not to "label" them (124:11). On the other hand, 40 per cent of these institutions did note the potential of low achievers by admitting them as probationary students, placing the students on guard and alerting the faculty.

There is absolutely no agreement of terminology when referring to students who are assigned to remedial courses. As previously stated, most of the community colleges avoid the problem by admitting and identifying these students as "regular" students, with the understanding that they must remedy certain deficiencies. It is from this point that much confusion ensues.

Since the mid-1950's, there has been evidence of a growing concern with the low achiever in community junior colleges. Rapidly increasing enrollments in recent years have served to emphasize the problem. Indeed, discussion has ensued as to whether the community college has an obligation to the low-achieving student. With pressures from society to lengthen the educational experience of all students, the low-achieving student has become conspicuous in community junior colleges. No semantical niceties will cover or hide the issue. No matter what the student is called, his problem is the same. To the extent that community junior colleges can identify these students and provide meaningful educational experiences for them, the institution has implemented the concept of the open door. If students are so identified and then allowed to fail, the community junior college has adopted a revolving door.

THE
TEACHERS

chapter 4 Who teaches the remedial student in the community junior college? Reports of programs for remedial students indicate that most members of a department in which remedial programs are offered are involved with at least one remedial course. Instructors typically are assigned a remedial course as part of their regular teaching load if they are teaching in an area where remediation is part of the department's function. There is one exception, however. Sociological research has shown that there is something of a "pecking order" in most departments, based almost entirely on seniority and tenure at the institution. Tenured instructors get first choice in teaching advanced or specialized courses. Instructors with less experience and tenure are therefore assigned to teach those classes that are left. Bossone found that 55 per cent of the instructors who taught remedial English in the California public junior colleges had two years or less of teaching experience (15:12). Other research (81) corroborates Bossone's conclusion that the inexperienced instructor is the one most often found in the remedial classroom.

Instructors in the remedial programs typically have not been adequately prepared for the courses that they are required to teach. The instructors in these programs agree, for the most part, that they are learning about remedial students through an on-the-job process (15:13). The concern for adequate preparation is echoed in a recent report of the American Association of Junior Colleges (53:39). Community junior college instructors interviewed in this report wanted graduate schools to recognize the unique problems associated with teaching in a community junior college. These instructors felt that graduate schools should offer courses and experiences that would prepare the prospective teacher for effective teaching in an open-door institution (53). This statement indicates that adequate preparation in a graduate program would at least partially solve the problem of inexperienced instructors being assigned to remedial courses.

The typical community college faculty member is a subject matter specialist. His graduate education has developed his interests and abilities along a narrow spectrum. This faculty member is "academically inclined," finding his greatest satisfaction in transmitting the knowledge of his chosen discipline to able students who can comprehend and appreciate the discipline. This accounts in large part for the instructor's preference for teaching advanced and specialized courses. It affords him the opportunity to teach that about which he knows the most.

There are other problems associated with instructing low-achieving students in remedial courses. Instructors are concerned about "status" and being properly identified with higher education. To teach a remedial or developmental course does not identify them with higher education, whereas teaching specialized and advanced courses affords instructors personal and professional prestige. Many teachers assert that low-achieving students and the remedial programs necessitated by their presence are of little or no concern to them. To these instructors the students and programs are quite simply not "college level" (100:32).

The claim that remedial objectives are beneath the dignity of community junior college instructors reveals another dimension of the problem—a lack of understanding of the complexity and extent of the effort at remediation. S. N. Postlethwait refers to this problem when he discusses the patient who went to a family doctor who never took "hard-to-get-well" cases (77:52). Simply stated, these community college instructors want to teach students who are easy to teach. They want students who are "already motivated." The old adage that "college is here if you want to take advantage of it, kid" is still prevalent in community junior colleges. It is evidenced by the fact that while 91 per cent of the community colleges surveyed in a national study agree with the concept of the open door, only 55 per cent provide special remedial courses for their low-achieving students (125:22).

Instructors in remedial courses frequently do not indicate any knowledge or understanding of the basic objectives of the courses. The same vague and general objectives that accompany the course outlines are the ones most often given by instructors as their teaching objectives. Many instructors indicate that their "primary objective" is to bring the student up to the level of the college credit course (15:14).

Another problem is identified as one of semantics. Instructors delight in the use of jargon. Terms like "college level" and "college material" abound on the community junior college campus. What is meant by teaching at the "college level"? Which students have been

17

identified as "college material"? What does "college material" mean? While some teachers appear genuinely concerned about the high rate of attrition in remedial programs, many simply explain the student dropout rate as proof that the students were not "college material" (76). Educational jargon is covering many of the problems that relate to teaching and learning in programs for low-achieving students.

The teacher is, without question, the most important element in the success of remedial programs (1:62-63). It has been reported that "25 per cent of the students in a class will fail if the teacher thinks they should, no matter what the program is" (19). This is most discouraging in light of evidence that not enough qualified instructors can be brought into an effective working force to provide for the academic needs of such students. There appears to be a real gap between what the junior college instructor views his role and function to be and what his role and function must be if the community junior college is to make good on its promise of providing educational opportunity for all.

While the defined tasks of the university faculty member include teaching, it is essentially subordinate to his other functions (11:144). The main purpose of the junior college instructor, however, is to teach. The junior college instructor, by virtue of his role, should be committed to a broad field of teaching, and also to a specialization in instructional processes (27:21). The junior college instructor is not expected to conduct research but he is supposed to engage in a deliberate effort to help all students learn.

Having a master's degree in a subject area does not insure that an instructor is a specialist in instructional processes. To the contrary, more often than not, it means that he knows very little about instructional processes. Few currently practicing instructors had any pedagogical preparation (28). In short, community junior college faculty members are ill prepared for the problems created by the open-door policy of admissions.

Several community colleges have recognized this problem. In the development of its program for low-achieving students, Bakersfield Junior College seriously considered the possibility of employing an outstanding *elementary teacher* to teach in its remedial program. The idea was abandoned, however, because it was feared that the teacher might take a "maternalistic view" of the program and overlook the screening function anticipated for the course (86:2).

Los Angeles City College has conducted evaluation studies of its program for remedial students over a period of years. These studies indicated that faculty training, experiences, and role expectations were not congruent with the instructional and personal-psychological demands made on them by the growing pressures of the "new remedial student." This institution recommended that specialized faculty members were needed to properly instruct the low-achieving students in the remedial programs. Research at Los Angeles City

College indicated that an experimental approach to the assignment of students and faculty based on personality, motivation, and certain attitudinal and/or intellectual characteristics would have value in establishing a positive learning climate (143:91).

Specific recommendations at Los Angeles City College included:

1. The development of in-service training programs on college time for faculty members to receive special training in the teaching and counseling of low-achieving students

2. The establishment of "group sessions" of faculty members working in this program to discuss and develop means to handle common problems: feelings and attitudes about the students; feelings and attitudes about their own aspirations and roles; developing new teaching procedures; and making recommendations and evaluations

3. The organization of seminars, symposiums, and workshops on the problems of teaching the remedial student (143:92).

Los Angeles City College is endeavoring to produce a teaching specialist, one who specializes in student learning. There is a great need for innovation in remedial instruction in community junior colleges because of their unique commitment; they constitute the only form of graded education in America in which attendance is voluntary, yet available to all who care to enroll. Instructors in remedial programs must become specialists in learning if the community college is to implement the concept of the open door (27:23).

A special workshop on programs for low achievers listed the following qualifications needed by instructors in remedial programs:

1. The instructor must seek change in the present curriculum or ignore it.

2. The instructor must understand his teaching field, but more important, he should be able to present the material at the level of the students.

3. The instructor must be willing to live with the knowledge that many people believe such students have no place in college.

4. The instructor must give up the belief that to be nonverbal is to be a nonlearner.

5. The instructor must believe in the educational worth of the remedial student.

6. The instructor must be willing to give up his subject-centered orientation in favor of involving himself with the student in relevant educational experiences which stress the processes by which learning takes place (1:62-63).

Although teacher attitudes and skills may be theoretically and empirically relevant to student success, how are these qualities to be developed? In-service workshops? Preservice preparation? Different forms of teacher selection prior to employment or differential assignments within the college? Utilizing teachers who can particularly help low-achieving students may be a step in the right direction, but can junior colleges arrange for them to achieve the appropriate recognition from their colleagues and status within their fields? Must teachers themselves be stimulated by superior students or can a breed of learning specialists be developed? These questions must be considered if community junior colleges are to make progress toward remediating academic deficiencies of the current generation of students. Automated teaching devices may solve many of the problems in time but, for now, the teacher is the key.

THE
OBJECTIVES

chapter 5 Educators agree that education serves as the medium through which culture is transmitted and through which individuals are socialized. And junior college remedial courses also help to attain this general educational goal. There is, however, no consensus on specific goals toward which remedial programs are pointed. Junior college administrators and others cannot even agree on the tangible objectives of remedial education, much less on a program that would meet the objectives.

Junior college leaders insist that remedial programs are developed and offered to remedy student deficiencies, to provide a second chance, and to salvage human resources. These concepts are rather altruistic in design and are consistent with the American dream of universal education. Individuals who have written about the junior college have ascribed other terms to the role and task of the two-year college. The words "cooling out," "providing a custodial function," and "implementing a filling station concept" are familiar to anyone who has read a recent textbook on the community junior college. These terms differ from the altruistic concepts listed above in two ways—they are more descriptive of what actually happens to students in the junior college and they have direct relevance to program design.

What does the term "remediation" mean? Perhaps the problem of setting objectives and goals for remedial courses is such a difficult one because individuals and institutions have not defined precisely what remediation is or what its goals should be. In general terms, however, remediation means making up—remedying—student deficiencies. Remediation implies that an institution is attempting to get a student from where he is to where he wants to be. It conveys the image of providing students with a second chance.

Those who advocate a "second chance" as a program objective maintain that education in a public junior college should be available to all who can profit from it. Few disagree with this concept for it is in keeping with the tradition of extending educational opportunities to all. The importance of such opportunities was clearly demonstrated after World War II when large numbers of veterans returned to college campuses throughout the country. Many of these individuals had been mediocre or failing students before entering military service; however, a majority of those who returned to school held clearly defined objectives and high levels of motivation. While colleges must maintain a certain degree of institutional integrity, this does not justify denying individuals a second chance in an appropriate educational program. Society cannot afford to cast aside individuals who may, given the opportunity, achieve a higher level of personal, academic, and occupational competence than they had in late adolescence; rather, society should encourage all individuals to learn to the limits of their abilities (11:274). The main question is whether these courses do, in fact, provide a second chance for students.

Undeniably, levels of student maturity and motivation play very important roles in the lives of young people who, for one reason or another, either stay in school or drop out. The community junior college can provide a second chance for those students who failed to complete high school. A second chance is also afforded those students whose grades and test scores in high school were poor and who, as a result, could not be admitted to a four-year college or university. The concept of "second chance" is closely tied to the programs for low-achieving students that are being offered in community colleges. In fact, remedial programs are the key to the success of the entire "second-chance" idea. Remedial courses and programs conceivably provide students with that second chance— if it can be effectively demonstrated that deficiencies have been remedied. By removing deficiencies, a student can feasibly pursue a program of interest to him. That junior colleges afford a second chance is directly related to the remedial offerings of the institution.

Closely related to the idea of providing a second chance is the view that community colleges "salvage human resources." Various writers in the field have identified the major function of the junior college remedial program as "salvaging" (134:43). Current dropout rates in high schools are alarming—25 per cent of all students who enter the ninth grade do not graduate. School dropout causes a problem which is compounded by the fact that there are increasing numbers of highly skilled and responsible jobs with ever-growing requirements for more sophisticated education and training. It has been predicted that by 1970 over 90 per cent of the jobs in our society will require a high school education or better (134:43). This view of the salvage function implies that the community college is salvaging individuals for the good of society in general. It implies that education is, indeed, a matter of national necessity—that the individual is worthy of salvage if for no other reason than that there will be unemployment if he is not.

Those who emphasize the salvage function correctly point to the need of an educated citizenry in a democratic society. Both concepts justify the "salvage" function from a societal viewpoint. Curiously, few writers justify "salvaging human resources" for the sake of the individual concerned.

The terms "remediation," "second chance," and "salvaging" are all closely related. Implications for the remedial program are the same, no matter which terms are used. By assigning these objectives to their remedial programs, one might suppose that community colleges would be anxious to demonstrate that they are being met.

Other objectives have been identified with the societal functions of the community college. Terms such as "custodial," "cooling out," and "filling station" have been used to describe what happens to students in the community junior college. The remedial offerings are directly related to these tasks.

Individuals have long identified certain junior college remedial programs as being "custodial" [137:27]. Society has delegated certain responsibilities to education in general and to the community college in particular. It has been maintained that junior colleges provide programs for low-achieving students in order to keep these young people out of the labor market, off the streets, and out of trouble. Most of the students in this category are assigned to an ordinary remedial course or program. The junior college has custody of the students concerned, but the programs that are provided are the same ones offered to all low-achieving students in the college.

How the custodial role should be properly implemented is a matter of conjecture. Some writers insist that the community college cannot be a quality educational institution and, at the same time, a custodial institution (11:273). Others say that a custodial function is within the purposes of the community college if useful educational programs are provided (137:28).

Another pragmatic objective or function is "cooling out," a term familiar to all junior college educators (25:71). The term is borrowed from gambling, specifically the confidence game. A confidence man, having fleeced a victim, must occasionally face the responsibility of allowing the victim to recognize the reality of his situation. In education, the term is used to suggest that the junior college has somewhat the same responsibility to its students—a responsibility to assist them in facing the reality of the difficult situation in which they often find themselves. It means assisting students in choosing courses that they can handle when their aspirations are illusory and above their ability (24:569-576). Slowly but surely, the student finds

23

out that he cannot pursue programs in his chosen area, and he modifies his educational choices as a result of the "cooling out" process.

Features of the "cooling out" process include advising students to take substitute courses that are not too different from the courses given up—particularly in status. Thus, in choosing an alternate course, the student does not fail, but rectifies a mistake (25:165-166) and is gradually disengaged from his chosen field, because he realizes that his abilities are inappropriate for his original choice. Counselors contribute to the "cooling out" process by helping students reduce educational aspirations and find other curricular areas in which to fulfill them. It is the counselor who brings the student to an awareness of his difficult situation.

Are remedial programs designed to "cool out" students? Some junior colleges frankly assert that they are. Other junior college educators, however, deny the "cooling out" process as an intended outcome of their remedial programs. It may be a by-product of an unsuccessful effort at remediation, but not an objective for a specific program.

The implications of "cooling out" for the community junior college remedial program are quite serious. "Cooling out" implies that two-year colleges do not want the responsibility of assisting students in making a *realistic* choice of educational goals as they enter the open door. It means that the student is either "cooled out" or "dropped out." And research shows that the latter is more often the case.

To some, community college remedial programs serve a "filling station" function (11:129). Simply stated, students enroll in these programs to achieve limited and immediate objectives—objectives with which the institution and instructor are unfamiliar. The student who enrolls in a remedial course usually views the course as a means to another end. The remedial program, therefore, exists to meet a limited educational objective for those students who actually prefer and intend to pursue college credit courses.

The implications of a "filling station" concept are quite clear: remedial courses must be viewed as a means to an end, and not as an end in themselves. Perhaps other courses and programs are necessary to adequately "fill" the educational objectives of students who do not want to enroll in regular college credit courses.

In summary, it seems that there is no agreement on objectives. In fact, there is a question regarding means-end distinctions. Are remedial courses means, remedying defects so that the student may go on to "college-level" work? Or are they ends, holding the student off the streets until he "cools out"—gets the message that college is not for him? Can they be both at the same time? Some writers vehemently reject a "custodial" function (11:273). Junior college teachers are embarrassed at the thought of a "cooling out" process. Others in the junior college quite simply deny that remediation is a function of the two-year college. They maintain that an open-door policy does not necessarily imply that remediation is a function of the junior college. Salvaging human resources and giving students a second chance are also controversial topics among various groups in the junior college.

Discussions of low-achieving students and available remedial programs are fraught with controversy. Some authorities emphasize that in the American scheme of things, there must always be remedial opportunities because the American philosophy is from the bottom up, not the top down (124:20). As a result, in the final analysis, junior colleges must decide what remedial programs are supposed to do and how best to implement the objective. Yet, it appears that goals and objectives for remedial programs are nebulous and ill defined because no one is absolutely convinced that it is even possible to remediate.

Research is needed to evaluate current programs and to point the way for more effective institutional efforts in the future.

THE PROGRAMS

chapter 6 Remedial courses for low-achieving students are offered in most community junior colleges throughout the nation. The low-achieving student is a challenge common to most community junior colleges, and the challenge will become more important and complex as increasing numbers of the population seek opportunities for higher education. The challenge is a natural consequence of the open-door admissions policy.

What are the courses offered? A survey of junior colleges in California indicated that most institutions offer similar courses, with different numbers, to meet institutional efforts at remediation (118:11). A recent study of the remedial course offerings in thirty-five California junior colleges indicated that more remedial courses were offered in English than in any other single subject area. All schools surveyed offered some type of remedial English course, while the majority of the schools offered several different types and levels of courses (118:11).

Paul Roman found that colleges recognized the importance of basic reading ability in all areas of college work. The emphasis of remedial reading courses was on improving basic reading habits, including those of word recognition, eye span, speed of comprehension, retention, and phonics. In some remedial reading courses, practice was afforded in scanning, finding essential ideas, idea associations, drawing inferences, analysis of reading defects, vocabulary work, and critical reading. Many schools reported a number of courses that provide the low achiever with some sequence of the life experiences that will hopefully enable him to live a more productive life as a citizen. Twenty-four of the colleges surveyed offered remedial mathematics courses. Eleven of the institutions offered some type of course in the social sciences, which included history, sociology, or political science. Only five of thirty-five community junior colleges offered remedial courses in the business area. However, there were numerous miscellaneous courses available for the low-achieving student (118:11-14).

Courses in California community colleges seem to be typical of current efforts elsewhere in which individual courses are offered to remedial students. Some institutions, however, have developed well considered total programs for low-achieving students. The total program approach is characterized by carefully defined objectives and study of student outcomes. Five such programs—those of Bakersfield, Compton, Contra Costa, Los Angeles City, and Forest Park Community Colleges will be considered in this chapter. Selection of the institutions whose programs will be considered here was based on the fact that they have not only defined their goals, but have actually written up their programs and, to some degree, evaluated them.

BAKERSFIELD COLLEGE —PROGRAM O

Over ten years ago, Bakersfield College found that regular college credit courses were enrolling increasing numbers of students with low academic potential. Research conducted at the college demonstrated that the presence of these students in regular college classes tended to impede the progress of other students. To remedy this problem, the college established Program O (the O stands for Opportunity), a one-semester program designed especially for the low-achieving student.

The envisioned purposes of Program O were: (1) to identify, as soon as possible, students of low academic potential or achievement; (2) to provide opportunity for these students to repair deficiencies and to demonstrate that they can do college work; (3) to remove the students who need remedial help from regular college classes in order that the progress of regular students would not be impaired; (4) to eliminate early those who could not succeed in regular college classes (87).

Program O operates as follows. Prior to registration, all entering students take the School and College Ability Test (SCAT) and an English classification test. Students scoring below approximately the tenth percentile on the tests are required to enroll in Program O classes. If a student's high school record is at wide variance with his test scores, he may, at the counselor's discretion, enroll in a regular college credit program.

There are three Program O classes: English 080, American Programs 080, and Mathematics 080. A student's test scores may qualify him for one, two, or three of these classes. Students who qualify for two or more 080 courses are assigned to a special counselor, are notified that they are entering on probation, and by means of special orientation sections, plus individual counseling conferences, are

27

afforded individual assistance in succeeding in their postsecondary endeavors. If students enrolled in Program O fail to maintain a 1.5 grade point average during their first semester of attendance, they are subject to dismissal from the college; if a 1.5 grade point average *is* achieved, the student is removed from probation. However, students must earn a grade of C or better in the remedial classes to which they have been assigned before progressing to the next level of instruction in the field. Each of the Program O courses carries three units of credit, but none of them meets graduation requirements in a subject field.

Students enrolled in Program O at Bakersfield College during the past ten years have had the following characteristics: On Stanford Achievement Tests, a mean score at grade 5.9 in spelling; grade 6.0 in reading comprehension; grade 7.6 in vocabulary; and grade 6.9 in overall reading. On the California Test of Mental Maturity, their mean IQ is 85. On the Los Angeles Public School Test of Mathematics Ability, the mean score is at grade 5.7. Students testing into Program O may be high school graduates with low academic ability, non-high school graduates, students with weak high school backgrounds, able students whose attitudes have prevented achievement, or students for whom English is, in reality or in effect, a foreign language.

By necessity, the instruction in these classes starts at about the fifth-grade level. The instruction quickly moves to about seventh-eighth grade level in mathematics (fractions, decimals, percentage), and to about eighth-ninth grade level in English (basic mechanics of English grammar). It is more difficult to ascribe a grade level to the introduction in American problems, but the course is taught at about eighth-grade level, although the discussion reflects the student's chronological maturity. A student receives a passing grade of C or higher in these courses if his work demonstrates that he can probably succeed in the lowest level regular college credit courses.

Extensive follow-up research has provided the college with a realistic appraisal of the degree of retention that can be expected from Program O students. Table I presents the retention rate over a three-year period of a typical group of students who entered Program O in the fall of 1959. Table II indicates the success of Program O in preparing students for admission to regular college credit courses.

The data show the number and percentage of Program O students who were considered good prospects for entering the regular college program for the second semester. It will be noted that the percentage of students who received permission to register for the spring semester increased steadily from 1958 through 1965, with a low of twenty-eight in 1958 to a high of sixty-three in 1962. In short, more and a greater percentage of students who begin Program O persist in it.

Table I:
RETENTION OF
PROGRAM O
STUDENTS

Retention

Number entering, fall 1959 98
  Average units attempted   13.3
  Average units completed   12.9
  Average G.P.A.   1.23

Number continuing, spring 1960 . . . . 46 = 47%
  Average units attempted   13.0
  Average units completed   10.3
  Average G.P.A.   1.57

Number continuing, fall 1960 . . . . 27 = 28%
  Average units attempted   12.5
  Average units completed   10.7
  Average G.P.A.   1.71

Number continuing, spring 1961 . . . . 22 = 22%
  Average units attempted   12.0
  Average units completed   10.8
  Average G.P.A.   1.53

Number continuing, fall 1961 . . . . 20 = 20%
  Average units attempted   8.8
  Average units completed   7.0
  Average G.P.A.   1.44

Number continuing, spring 1962 . . . . 12 = 12%
  Average units attempted   10.7

Candidates for graduation, spring 1962 . . . . . . 4 = 4%

Table II:
CHARACTERISTICS
OF STUDENTS
IN PROGRAM O

	1958	1959	1960	1961	1962	1963	1964	1965
Total number of students tested	1654	1647	1638	1852	1903	1962	2413	2850
Number of students testing for Program O . . .	149	172	184	168	210	179	231	203
Percentage testing for Program O	9	10	11	9	11	9	9.5	7
Midterm G.P.A. (total)	—	1.32	1.40	1.47	1.43	1.66	1.52	1.47
Average IQ (CTMM)	80.6	86.0	86.9	86.3	88.0	83.2	—	—
Number of students approved to register after one semester	25	39	40	58	60	62	72	81
Per cent approved to register	28	39	41	54	42	63	48	55

Two factors identified by the college account for this marked increase:

1. A more effective individualized program of counseling Program O students, and

2. A more effective Program O instructional program, developed and modified after years of research in the program.

Evaluation of Program O has been continuous since its inception. Research at Bakersfield College on the effectiveness of its program has led to the following conclusions:

1. Approximately 30 per cent of the students who enroll in any Program O class will receive a grade of C or higher.

2. Ability is only one of the critical criteria of success with this group. However, an IQ of 90 or above is positively correlated with academic success in Program O.

3. The program is highly dependent upon sensitive and competent counseling and instruction (87).

The Bakersfield research has produced agreement on one point: An arbitrary cut-off score on the School and College Ability Test (SCAT) does not adequately identify the students for whom Program O was designed. It is obvious that SCAT scores in themselves are inadequate measures of the deficiencies that Program O is designed to remedy.

Program O is a program conceived and designed by Bakersfield College to solve the problems of the remedial student. It is an institutional effort to provide educational opportunities for all students entering the open door. The program was not easily designed or simply implemented. College counselors report that the most serious problem in implementing Program O was developing faculty support for the project, yet faculty support was essential since few programs can succeed without it. Today, Program O seems to have this support.

COMPTON JUNIOR COLLEGE The program at Compton Junior College in South Central Los Angeles (the Compton-Watts-Willowbrook area which gained national prominence during the 1965 riots), is illustrative of an institution's response to the demands placed on a junior college in an urban area. Indeed, Compton's example yields insight into what a community junior college can do when two-thirds of its entering population score below the fortieth percentile on the School and College Abilities Test (SCAT). Compton was forced to move away from traditionally oriented curriculums in order to attempt to establish an entirely new approach that would reflect and implement the "salvage" function of the two-year college.

What did Compton do? Early in 1963 the college president directed the dean of instruction to develop, with the assistance of appropriate faculty committees, broad outlines for major changes in matriculation procedures and course content. Basically, Compton was seeking ways of developing programs that would provide basic education in addition to job training. The programs were to be based on the assumption that traditional vocational-technical courses alone were not the answer for young people, that there were no easy answers, and that they could hope only that their best efforts would at least scratch the surface of the problem.

The Compton group designed a program that would take the student at his educational level, discover his strengths and weaknesses, analyze his potential, and place him in learning situations where he not only had a chance to succeed but where he could also develop his capacities for useful citizenship. Moreover, Compton designed the program to keep the student in school for a reasonable period of time, recognizing that it was not possible to correct a lifetime of deficiencies in one semester. In its broadest sense, the program was an attempt to acculturate students into the mainstream of American life. What made it distinct from traditional programs was the philosophy behind it and the determination to develop classes in all areas of the campus that represented a true equality of opportunity, an opportunity for the student to enter *and* remain in school and, of most importance, an opportunity to move from one level of achievement to a higher one.

CHARACTERISTICS OF THE COMPTON PROGRAM

The Compton program is characterized by the following:

1. All courses have been developed with full faculty cooperation.

2. Courses are established in regular departments using regular classroom facilities and regular faculty members who also teach traditional college classes.

3. Subject matter is geared to the young adult who is taught at an academic level commensurate with his present attainments.

4. Each class follows a regular course of instruction with emphasis on:

a. Development of favorable work habits in conscientious sustained effort

b. Accumulation of factual information and vocabulary deemed important to success in more advanced study

c. Opportunity for discussion and consideration of special problems and value judgments.

5. Each student is required to take at least one course in basic English.

6. Every class involves some writing, general vocabulary development, and other language skills.

7. Classical "dumbbell" approaches are studiously avoided.

8. Efforts are made to "lift up" the student rather than "talk down" to him.

9. Efforts are made to include in every course some attention to citizenship, social responsibility, intelligent voting practices, academic and vocational opportunities available, and acceptable standards of reliability, dependability, punctuality, and loyalty to democratic institutions (82).

As part of the process of matriculation, all students enrolling at the college are required to take placement examinations, the SCAT and the Purdue Placement Test in English. Students are placed according to the following classifications:

Level I: 89 and below on the Purdue and 10 per cent and below on the SCAT total score

Level II: 90 - 119 on the Purdue and 11 - 39 on the SCAT total score

Level III: 120 and above on the Purdue and 40 per cent and above on the SCAT total score (82).

In instances where a student's score crosses classifications, the counselor has the privilege of determining placement according to collected data. For example, high verbal scores may be attained in some cases along with low levels in quantitative factors, or the situation may be reversed. In these cases, scholarship and training in high school may be weighed with the test scores in the counselor's recommendations for the student's program.

LEVEL I STUDENTS

Level I students receive only provisional status. They are non-high school graduates or high school graduates with grade point averages of 2.0 or lower. Furthermore, they may be applicants lacking a high school or college transcript or they may simply be students scoring at or below the tenth percentile on the SCAT. Students in the Level I category usually score below 90 on the Purdue test and are, consequently, placed in Communications 200, a remedial English course. Their programs are limited to 12½ units in addition to physical education and they are allowed to elect subjects from any of the courses numbered in the 200 series. In a few instances, however, specifically in skill areas or in other fields where satisfactory high school work enables him to meet certain prerequisites, the student is permitted to elect courses in Level II.

LEVEL II STUDENTS

Level II students are enrolled in a program that provides primarily for vocational preparation and they often attain the A.A. or A.S. degree. They are also given the opportunity to qualify for the transfer program by doing remedial work and completing necessary course prerequisites.

Students in the Level II program are limited to 15½ units, 7 of which may be remedial English—Subject A, English B (reading), and English E (spelling and vocabulary improvement)—depending on their scores on the Purdue examination. Placement of students depends on their individual preparation, their educational and vocational plans, their ability to meet course prerequisites, and their counselors' recommendations.

LEVEL III STUDENTS

Level III students are offered the opportunity to take courses for transfer to a four-year college or university or to complete vocational training which will prepare them for employment at the end of their fourteenth year. These students are usually permitted to take 17½ units in their first semester and they concentrate either on fulfilling university requirements for the first two years, or they devote their time to training for specific vocations. Moreover, these students may combine university or vocational preparation with attainment of the A.A. degree.

THE PROGRAM

After a Level I student completes 12 units of work with a grade point average of C or better, he remains in Level I, but is classified as a regular student. He is then allowed to take any course in the curriculum—provided he has qualified for the prerequisites. If the student receives a B or an A in Communications 200, he may elect to take the placement tests again. If he scores below 90 on the Purdue test, he is required to complete Communications 201. If he scores between 90 and 119, he must take English A, the regular college credit course. If his score is 120 or above, he qualifies for English 31 A. Other selections in his course of study depend on his major, his vocational and educational plans, his quantitative scores on the SCAT, and his ability to meet course prerequisites.

If the Level I student earns a grade of C or less in Communications 200, he has no option to repeat the entrance tests—he must complete Communications 201. The remaining courses in his program will probably be selected again from others in the 200 series unless he is able to meet course prerequisites elsewhere. At the end of the first semester, as with other students, if he fails to maintain a grade point average of 1.5, he is placed on scholastic probation. At the end of the year, if his over-all average is still less than 2.0, he is continued on probation; if his average falls below 1.5, he is disqualified from the program.

A Level II student who desires eventual transfer to a four-year college may qualify for English 31 A by making a C in Subject A. The grade also entitles him to enter other transfer courses which require satisfactory verbal ability.

Students in Levels II and III also may qualify for the A.A. degree after they complete the necessary 60 units, attain a C average, and fulfill the basic course requirements in English, history, health, science, fine arts, and physical education.

The Compton program can be summarized quite aptly by the philosophy motivating it: "The open-door policy of California public junior colleges places the burden for salvaging human talent whenever possible on this segment of higher education (the junior college)." The Compton staff shares the responsibility for giving each student ample opportunity to demonstrate the true quality of his scholastic work before closing the door to further study in an institution of higher education. The program (1) provides curriculums that will meet the needs of the total student body, (2) permits the counselors to develop a more flexible arrangement of courses designed to move the student toward his educational objective, (3) provides a

33

more complete program for the student who must combine remedial work with his regular program, (4) lessens the number of students on scholastic probation and disqualification and minimizes the drop-out problem, resulting in better retention, (5) affords a more homogeneous grouping in college transfer classes, (6) offers a place for the student in vocational technology classes to study general education at a level in which he can succeed, and, finally, (7) yields an opportunity to the adult whose educational background is meager to attend a school with a program designed to cater to his needs (82).

CONTRA COSTA JUNIOR COLLEGE

Contra Costa Junior College adopted a new—indeed, revolutionary—approach to solving the problem of remedial programs. In a pilot project begun in March 1966, Contra Costa created a tutoring program to determine the effectiveness of tutoring as a means of meeting the needs of its low-achieving students.

Philosophically, the program assumes that the low-achieving student enters the college with social, economic, and educational handicaps which do not reflect his true potential as a student, but, instead, are evidence of a multiple alienation which frustrates his personal development. The major premise is that, barring a major change in junior college curriculums, the most expedient and practical solution for remedial students is to supplement their course work with an extensive tutoring program. Inherent in the program is the assumption that tutoring works—that it is effective—for in the tutoring situation, unlike the classroom, students have the freedom to ask questions and to go back over material without fear of embarrassment or impeding the schedule of the lesson. In the tutoring situation, a relationship develops and learning acquires personality, thereby eliminating alienation as a factor.

The program, which is outlined below, seeks to develop tutoring as a major means of meeting the problems of the remedial student—remedying his deficient reading, writing, and mathematical skills—his alienation from learning. The program assumes that the so-called "salvage" function of the junior college has the negative connotation of repairing something nearly ruined and almost worthless. Instead, the tutoring program has a *discovery* function: the revelation of strong and valuable resources in the student that have been submerged or repressed. The tutoring program was designed to accommodate subject matter *and* personality (30).

ADMINISTRATION OF THE TUTORING PROGRAM

The tutoring program administration is composed of two bodies: a program coordinator and an advisory board. The advisory board is responsible for program direction, evaluation, recommendations, and consultation with the program coordinator. Meetings with the program coordinator are held twice a month to review progress reports, and include all individuals who contribute significantly to the program. Responsibility for appointing members of the selection-evaluation and research committee administering the program rests with the program coordinator. He also determines day-to-day operating procedures and records the data for evaluation.

SELECTION OF TUTORS

Potential tutors file applications for employment with the tutoring program. They are required to write statements discussing their educational experiences, backgrounds, interests, abilities, and ideas about teaching and tutoring. Although competence as a student is an essential factor in selecting tutors, the candidate's eligibility is not determined solely by an outstanding grade point average, for not all outstanding students make good teachers and not all good teachers were outstanding students. Thus, the candidate is required to have a solid C average and a demonstrated ability in one academic or terminal area. He must have at least two letters of recommendation, one from his counselor and one from a teacher in his area of specialization. He is also asked to submit other letters of recommendation or any other information which he feels will strengthen his application.

Next, the candidate for tutoring is interviewed by the selection-evaluation committee. He is judged on the basis of his (1) ability to speak knowledgeably of subject material, (2) enthusiasm, (3) effectiveness in communicating ideas, and (4) effectiveness in establishing rapport with the board.

TRAINING AND ORIENTATION OF TUTORS

In the Contra Costa Program, there are two types of tutors. One type tutors the student throughout the semester, while the other instructs the tutor at the beginning of each semester. As part of their education, the tutors are taught most methods of education and they learn about student learning.

The continuing education of the tutor consists of three or four hours a month of seminar with instructors in the areas of math and English. These seminars are held for tutors specializing in the particular area, though all are invited to attend. Seminar leaders serve as "troubleshooters" for any problems that the tutors have with their courses or their materials. In this way, tutors have continuous contact with students and faculty in the areas in which they are tutoring. In terms of teaching the tutor to work with his prospective students, the best method used is to "tutor the tutor"—to expose him to the same kind of teaching that he will be doing. The audience of tutors carefully observes all the verbal and nonverbal communication that takes place. The tutor is shown the various devices available to him for effective teaching: the use of plastic structures, blocks, tinker toys, etc., to indicate whole numbers and fractions, addition, subtraction, multiplication, and division; the audiovisual devices available to him such as opaque projectors, tape recorders for recording recitation of the speech difficulties which often compound writing problems; and the textbooks and other sources of information that he can use for reference.

35

Tutors work a maximum of fifteen hours a week, although only ten of these hours are spent with their students—the remaining five are used to record grades and maintain data on students. Furthermore, they work on a one-to-one basis with their students as the semesters begin. Once the one-to-one relationship is established, however, the tutor may work with several students who have similar problems, thereby allowing him to develop a sense of community and confidence in and between each of his students (30).

When the original report of Contra Costa's Tutoring Program was published, the program was still in the germination stage. At the time of this writing, a follow-up report had not yet been produced.

LOS ANGELES CITY COLLEGE

Los Angeles City College experienced much of what the other institutions discussed earlier experienced—growing numbers of low-achieving students entering the college and, increasingly, students being disqualified from various programs. As a result, faculty and administration decided that the college was not fulfilling its responsibility to the remedial student. Studies conducted by the counseling office revealed that approximately 7,000 students took the entrance examination annually and that 20 per cent, or 1,400 of them, placed below the eleventh percentile on national college freshman norms. Studies showed, too, that 60 per cent of these students dropped out by the end of their first semester, with doubtful educational benefit in the process.

In response to this challenge, former President John Lombardi adopted the policy of separating those students deemed incapable of doing regular college work on the basis of their SCAT scores and limiting them to ten units of especially selected introductory and remedial courses which were recommended by each instructional department. Moreover, the problem was referred to the committee of academic and scholarship standards, which recommended the development of an experimental program for those students. They decided that the program should involve extensive testing, use of programed materials, cutting across subject-matter lines where desirable, and experimenting with team teaching and other innovative teaching methods. Administrative coordination of the program was assigned to the counseling center under a committee composed of the assistant dean, the research coordinator, and a retired faculty member. Teaching faculty were recruited on a voluntary basis from experienced, enthusiastic, and sympathetic instructors.

The objectives of the program were to:

1. Obtain information about the "low-achieving" student to see if some characteristics could be found which would identify the "salvageable" student

2. Identify methods and techniques of teaching and counseling which would make it possible to remedy the disadvantage of the student in one semester

3. Impart to the student those skills and that knowledge which would aid him in finding a place for himself in society (108).

THE INITIAL EXPERIMENT

Initially, the experiment consisted of enrolling sixty-four students who had scored below the eleventh percentile of national college norms on the SCAT in spring 1964. The students were enrolled in an English fundamentals and an introductory psychology course, each of which met for five hours a week. Instructors were given wide latitude in organizing time, curriculum, and materials. And the California State Department of Employment agreed to assist by administering vocational aptitude tests and informing students of vocational opportunities. For comparative purposes, a control group was also tested. The program was continued in the fall 1964, with 100 students and the addition of a speech class, thus increasing class hours to three each day (108).

Those teaching in the "block program," as it was dubbed, began to meet informally for coffee each Wednesday morning and they began to coordinate their offerings into an integrated experience for their students. For instance, while the English class was reading and discussing *The Red Badge of Courage*, the psychology instructor encouraged a study of the motives displayed by the characters in the book or developed role playing in similar situations, and the speech instructors encouraged debates and speeches on the same topics or examinations of various dialogues used in the book. Thus, during the school year, there was frequent interaction of the various forces affecting the curriculum. And, in the summer of 1965, after the program was in progress for a year, these forces came together and administrative decisions affecting the program were made.

First and foremost, the group decided that the program should be moved out of the experimental stage and into the operational phase, for its members were sure that the program was benefiting the students enrolled and that, simultaneously, it was facilitating the maintenance of high-quality education and scholastic standards. Second, it was decided that administrative control of the program should be shifted from the counseling center to the joint supervision of the dean of instruction and the dean of student personnel in order to encourage more extensive use of innovative methods and experimentation. Third, they decided that the program should be operated within the framework of the already existing departmental structure instead of as a separate division or extension of the college. Fourth, and most importantly, they decided that the *primary focus of the program should be shifted from remediation to general education because the evidence derived from extensive student testing indicated that progress was made in raising the reading level and academic ability of the students involved in the program, but that, except in a few instances, not enough progress could be made in a semester or a year to enable the student to move into regular college classes with a reasonable chance of success.* Inasmuch as most of the students would not continue at the college for more than a year, they decided to emphasize those things that would help the student to know himself and his potential better, accept realistic vocational goals, become a better citizen, and become more aware of his cultural heritage. Fifth, they decided to expand the program offerings from one semester to a year and to discontinue scholastic disqualification of students after only one semester of work. Sixth, they decided that the college should develop an instructional materials laboratory as soon as possible. Finally, seventh, they decided to ask for funds for experimentation from the Ford Foundation (108).

To implement the decisions, the dean of instruction organized a planning committee consisting of administrators, instructors, and department chairmen involved in the program. The committee recommended that the first-semester program for spring 1966 consist of:

Fundamentals of U.S. history and government	3 units	5 hours
English fundamentals	3 units	5 hours
Communication skills	3 units	5 hours
An elective in one of the special courses in art, business, home economics, mathematics, music, or psychology	3 units	3 hours
Physical education	$^1/_2$ unit	2 hours
	$12^1/_2$ units	20 hours

The committee also recommended that a second-semester program be planned by the counseling staff and submitted to the dean of instruction.

The counseling committee met and recommended that a special "core" course be developed for the second semester. It was proposed that the course should meet five hours a week and, in addition to the continued emphasis on reading, writing, and communication skills, it should include elements of personal finance, human relations, personal business etiquette, and health and nutrition. It was suggested, too, that up to six units of vocational courses recommended by a counselor and an elective from the list of restricted courses be included in the second semester.

Next, the dean of instruction, the dean of student personnel, the dean of admissions, and the counselors met to set up administrative controls so that students scoring at the tenth percentile or below on the SCAT would be routed into the special courses developed for them. It was, moreover, decided to continue the policy that students may not withdraw from any of the classes without dropping out of college completely.

EVALUATION   It is still too early to assess the success of Los Angeles City College's block program. In the spring 1966 semester there were 240 first-semester students and 140 second-semester students in the program.

The real test of the program began in the fall 1966 semester when it was expected that 80 students would qualify for the first semester and 200 would qualify for the second. Evaluation studies are under way at present.

FOREST PARK COMMUNITY COLLEGE

A faculty committee at Forest Park Community College, St. Louis, Missouri, in 1964 investigated the total college program and found the following: (1) 46 per cent of the on-campus enrollment, a total of 1,510, experienced academic difficulty; (2) enforced withdrawal was experienced by 278 students; (3) the number placed on academic probation was 318; and (4) 180 withdrew officially or stopped coming. With these results in mind, the faculty committee recommended an experimental program with four goals:

1. Meeting the needs of students in the lower range of the ability spectrum

2. Improving standards in transfer courses by removing students incapable of making a contribution or of achieving significant benefit

3. Providing educationally disadvantaged students with intensive counseling on an individual and group basis to: (a) minimize emotional factors inhibiting success; (b) aid students to assess realistically their potential and to relate this to vocational goals; and (c) identify students incapable of benefiting from any college program and refer them to community resources through accurate and complete knowledge of apprenticeship requirements, job openings, training courses such as those sponsored by the Manpower Development and Training Act, as well as other community resources

4. Salvaging the academically able students from this group who might be upgraded to the point where they could be successful in regular technical or transfer programs (117).

THE PROGRAM

Two patterns of curriculum were used: pattern A included economics and modern math; pattern B, sociology and biology. Both included English literature, communications skills, and counseling psychology. These curricular arrangements were offered to give remediation in the basic skills of writing and math and to develop more breadth in general education background.

Sixty-seven students were randomly assigned to pattern A, and sixty-eight to pattern B. Five staff members were assigned to each group of students, respectively referred to as team I and team II. Besides the bimonthly meetings of all ten staff members, each team's staff met as often as possible to consider placement, progress, morale, etc.

For the remediation of basic skills, a programed materials learning laboratory was opened. Students in the first semester of the program spend an average of six hours per week in the laboratory. Another characteristic of the program is its emphasis on placement. The three areas of placement are technical or transfer programs on cam-

39

pus, community training programs, and on-the-job placement. In addition to extensive individual and group counseling, placement information is obtained through classroom and laboratory observations and through a testing program which includes personal inventories and tests of interest and academic skills.

EVALUATION The program uses a pretest and posttest design with alternate forms for evaluation. General ability, general achievement, and basic academic skills are measured. Students who spend one semester in the program show a significant improvement on six of their ten posttest scores. Significant increases are achieved on the SRA Reading Placement Test, Wide Range Achievement Test (numerical), writing and social studies of the Sequential Tests of Educational Progress (STEP), and the verbal and total of the School and College Abilities Test (SCAT). Posttest scores on the reading, math, and science of STEP and numerical of SCAT do not show a significant increase. Thirty-two students who spent a complete year in the program experienced significant increases on the STEP math and SCAT numerical (136).

One hundred twenty-five of the original 135 completed the first semester. Nineteen did not return for the next semester. Twenty-one were recommended for a college transfer program, twenty-four for technical programs, fifty-seven to continue the general curriculum program, and four were recommended for developmental courses. Of the ten staff members, eight requested to remain in the program.

Application laboratories, planned for the fall of 1966, were added to the program to insure that skills learned in the specific conditions of the programed materials learning laboratory could be applied in other conditions.

SUMMARY The appeal of a total program approach to the low-achieving student is that it appears to have greater facility and potential for dealing with the complexity of the problem. Although complete evaluations of total programs for the low-achieving student are not available, there is indication that such programs are effective in retaining students beyond the first semester. That instructional effectiveness in total programs is superior to individual classes is not yet clear.

THE
RESEARCH

chapter 7 In the last decade there has been evidence of a growing concern in junior colleges with the remedial student. Rapidly increasing enrollments in recent years have served to emphasize the problem. Many two-year colleges practice an "open-door" admissions policy. Increasing numbers of full-time students in the community colleges are low-achieving students (124:22). Instructors are employed to teach these increasing multitudes of students, and courses are created to remedy student deficiencies. Terms like "salvage" and "second chance" are used to describe the efforts at assisting remedial students. Millions of dollars are expended annually on programs for these students. Indeed, programs and instructors for remedial students presently constitute a major institutional endeavor by the community colleges. Yet, with very few exceptions, little research has been implemented to evaluate the effectiveness of these programs and instructors.

Certain writers (24) have emphasized that it is most important that students and parents never become fully cognizant of what actually happens to students who enter the open-door college. This suggests that research on remedial program effectiveness is actually avoided—the implication being that if parents and taxpayers in general ever realized how ineffective the junior college has been with the low-achieving student, the entire institution would be in jeopardy. Has research been avoided to cover actual weaknesses in remedial programs? Or do junior college administrators and instructors assume that they are professionals and are therefore doing a good job? No definite answers are available to these questions, but one thing is clear: few institutions have bothered either to describe

41

or evaluate their programs for the low-achieving student. Intuition rather than research appears to be the basis for most remedial programs.

What research is available that evaluates the success of programs for the student enrolled in junior college remedial courses? This chapter will report recent findings in the following categories: surveys of remedial programs at the state and national level; objectives and functions of junior college remedial programs; faculty and student attitudes; class size and teaching procedures; the placement of students; student motivation; and grouping of students.

SURVEYS AT THE NATIONAL AND STATE LEVEL

A national study of courses and curriculums for low-achieving students found that, while 91 per cent of the junior colleges admit all high school graduates and all persons over eighteen years of age who could profit from the instruction, only 20 per cent have designed special curriculums for them. Community junior colleges apparently are attempting to meet the needs of low-achieving students by providing remedial courses which are typically available to all students (124:22). In fact, the regular remedial courses of the junior colleges are the only curricular offerings that are available for the majority of low-achieving students but, as several institutions have recently discovered, these remedial courses are frequently too difficult for the students who enroll in them (82).

A state survey in California found that remedial English classes in the California public junior colleges were not sufficiently effective (15:1). This investigation identified the following contributing factors that made the remedial classes ineffectual:

1. Questionable placement procedures
2. Lack of communication between those involved in testing or counseling and guidance and those involved in the teaching of remedial English
3. Oversized classes and overworked teachers
4. Inadequately trained teachers and generally unenthusiastic teachers
5. Outdated and superficial course outlines
6. Vague objectives
7. Lack of agreement about what should be taught in the course
8. Lack of suitable instructional materials
9. Confusion about proper methodology in remedial classes
10. Lack of knowledge about students' reading and writing abilities and interests
11. Lack of knowledge about students' personal problems, limitations, and preferences for methods and materials
12. Variety of highly subjective grading standards
13. Insufficient experimentation.

The study suggested that the confusion regarding remedial programs was directly related to the paucity of research on the subject.

It concluded that remedial programs and instructional processes have typically been organized on an intuitive basis (15:38). This "fly-by-the-seat-of-your-pants" approach is inadequate and inappropriate in light of the high attrition rates in remedial programs.

OBJECTIVES AND FUNCTIONS

Other research has demonstrated that the remedial function of the junior college is achieved only when the courses designed to fulfill this function are really remedial and help to provide students with the opportunity to remedy basic deficiencies. When courses have a remedial title but must also serve other functions, they do not fulfill the role for which they were established (145:5). This suggests that remedial programs must be designed specifically to remedy student deficiencies and nothing more. Objectives for other students must be met in other curricular programs.

Several institutional research reports have confirmed the need for courses and programs whose objectives are geared to the needs of the students enrolled in them. In an investigation of the success of its remedial program, Los Angeles City College found that the overwhelming majority of its low-achieving students did not persist in college for more than a year. Fewer than five in a hundred remedial students ever qualified for the transfer or the technical program at Los Angeles City College. The remedial program was not remedying student deficiencies to the point that they entered regular college credit courses; therefore, the emphasis was shifted to general education, defined as preparing students for life in contemporary society. Based on specific research findings, emphasis and content of programs for the remedial student were changed (60).

Forest Park Community College conducted an institutional research study to determine the gain in student academic achievement after one semester and after one year in its general curriculum program (a remedial program). The hypothesis tested was that low-achieving students who completed either one semester or one year in the general curriculum program would improve significantly on their posttest scores in (a) basic academic skills as measured by the SRA Reading Placement Test and the Wide Range Achievement Test (numerical only); (b) breadth of general education knowledge as measured by the Sequential Tests of Education Progress (STEP)—reading, writing, mathematics, social studies and science; and (c) general ability as measured by the School and College Ability Test (SCAT) (136:7).

The study found that general curriculum students showed a significant gain in basic academic skill levels. There was also a significant increase in verbal and total scores on the School and College Ability Test (SCAT) for both one-semester and one-year students. If program success were measured by significant gains made by students, the above data would support the contention that the program was quite successful. In this study, gains reached numerical significance, and yet there was little evidence that the level attained

43

on posttesting represented enough of an increase to warrant the transfer of the average one-semester or one-year general curriculum student to *any* technical or transfer program offered by the college (136:7). The posttest scores were still below the cut-off score required for students to enter the college credit programs.

Like Los Angeles City College, Forest Park Community College recommended that the general curriculum program be considered nonremedial in function. Rather, emphasis in the program would be given to cultural enrichment and job placement upon completion of the program. Specific research findings served as the vehicle for curriculum modification at Forest Park.

The significant finding stemming from both the Los Angeles and the Forest Park research is that student deficiencies were not being remedied. Students did not persist in or beyond the remedial programs. Neither investigation suggested reasons as to why the remedial programs failed, only that they failed.

A recent investigation compared the success of students enrolled in Bakersfield College's Program O with the success of students in another junior college where no special programs and/or counseling are provided for low-achieving students. Defining student grade point average as success, this investigation found little difference between the Program O students and the students enrolled as regular students in another California junior college. However, there was much greater student persistence in Bakersfield's Program O (124:149-150).

FACULTY AND STUDENT ATTITUDES

Faculty attitudes seem to be positively related to student success in remedial programs. Many investigations have reported that favorable attitudes toward the teaching of remedial students result in significantly higher student achievement (81:40). Teaching methods and procedures may also be related to student achievement, as reported in recent research. Discussion methods have been found superior to lecture methods in improving student scores on tests in remedial courses (43:329-335). Other research has indicated that student attitudes are improved in small-group sections (20:54). More important, studies by Casey and Weaver indicated that permanence of learning, which is the most crucial factor in any remedial course, is highly dependent upon the attitudes which the student develops. The study reinforces other data available on the importance of student attitudes in remedial programs. Students who perceive a remedial course with positive attitudes are more likely to retain and to use the material learned over a longer period of time than students who have negative attitudes and are affected by class size and teaching methods (20).

CLASS SIZE AND TEACHING PROCEDURES

Despite the lack of conclusive experimental support, many professors continue to believe that student achievement in small classes is superior to that in large classes (90:67-77). Recent investigations have found that large classes were about equal to smaller ones in covering course content, but were inferior in achieving other objectives. Several experimental studies have indicated that students have more positive attitudes toward the achievement of course objectives when small classes are utilized for remedial instruction (145:37).

According to some research findings, discussion is crucial for building positive student perceptions in remedial classes (145:38-39). A discussion approach involves a classroom which is characterized by extensive student participation, lack of consistent correction by the instructor, lack of excessive instructor direction, and most important, more discussion of ideas related to personal experiences. Moreover, students in courses relying upon textbook materials for remedial work do not show as extensive an improvement as do those in courses relying almost exclusively upon discussion, with textbooks used as reference sources, if at all. Student perceptions of the fulfillment of course objectives are also much higher when the discussion method is used as compared to the textbook approach (145:39). Supportive research indicates that students who are taught by the participative action method not only develop more effective attitudes toward remedial classes but also are superior in role flexibility and self-insight to those students taught by traditional methods (55:247).

Related research indicates that student perceptions of remedial courses are influenced positively by the use of audiovisual materials, provided that these materials are directly related to the achievement of course objectives. When instructors use films, filmstrips, recordings, and related materials only for the purpose of filling class time, however, negative attitudes increase more sharply in remedial classes than they do in regular college credit courses (145:34). The use of audiovisual materials, combined with immediate feedback of student learning, appears to be a most significant factor in shaping positive attitudes toward learning. It is also positively related to the possibility of the learner incorporating his learning into his daily behavior (145:34). Investigations have also reported that the use of programed materials results in higher student achievement, while more traditional instructional methods actually result in lower student achievement (81:39).

A programed method of instruction in English A (a remedial course) was recently introduced in the San Diego Junior Colleges (63). A pilot study was conducted to gain some indication of the relative performance of students receiving programed instruction. The general plan was to administer final examinations to experimental and control groups and to analyze the results. The study sample was selected from students enrolled in English A at Mesa College during the fall 1966 semester. The experimental group consisted of fifty-eight students who received programed instruction; the control group included fifty-eight enrollees not taught by the programed method. Final examinations were used as dependent variables. One type was designed primarily for the programed group while another test was selected for its appropriateness for the group not taught by the programed method. At the end of the semester each group took both tests and the results were compared by applying significance tests to observed differences in the means. The results of this study supported the hypothesis that students in English A who had received programed instruction would obtain significantly higher scores on the final examinations than those enrollees not taught by the programed method (63).

THE PLACEMENT OF STUDENTS

With few exceptions, test scores are the most used criterion for placing students in remedial programs. Yet available research indicates that there is little, if any, correlation between these scores and subsequent success in remedial programs (108). Indeed, some institutional research studies have shown that there is absolutely no correlation. Where test scores have been successfully used, it was in connection with other predictors, namely high school grade point averages and certain nonintellective factors. Available research tends to support the statement that test scores alone are not adequate predictors of student success in remedial programs.

While test scores are widely employed for placing students in remedial programs, they are rarely used to determine if students are eligible for admission to the regular college credit classes. Most typically, students are declared eligible for college credit classes on the basis of the grades they earned in remedial courses. In short, the criterion used for placing students in remedial programs is not typically used in evaluating student progress or in allowing them to enter regular college credit classes. Available research has shown that there is little relationship between student scores on placement tests and the grades that students subsequently earn in remedial courses (125:23).

STUDENT MOTIVATION

Student perception of remedial programs and instructional processes seems to be positively related to student achievement. Recent investigations have reported that individualized instruction is perceived by students as being an extremely critical factor in their achievement in remedial courses (141:285-286). Other research reports that student perceptions of remedial classes are heavily influenced by anxiety; that male students typically perceive these courses more negatively than do females, because males are more sensitive to the loss of status involved in taking a substandard course. Male students exhibiting high anxiety are the first to see the class as conflicting with their own personal motivations and the first to drop out of the course. These same students score the lowest on examinations and papers given in remedial classes, even though many of them are highly capable students, as measured by both the Scholastic Aptitude Test and the Standardized Wechsler Adult Intelligence Test. Females, whose motivation is more positive, tend to persist in remedial classes longer, work harder, achieve better grades, and evidence a more positive perception upon completion of the course (4:52-63).

GROUPING OF STUDENTS

The subject of homogeneous grouping is clouded by conflicting research reports. Several investigations have indicated that students who are grouped homogeneously tend to develop more positive perceptions of the course than do students grouped heterogeneously. Some investigations have supported this conclusion by maintaining that homogeneous grouping helps to reduce the competition in class. These investigations indicate that excessive competition with higher-achieving students is one of the major factors in undermining the remedial student's desire to learn (145:42).

Other researchers, however, have indicated that homogeneous groupings are not superior to heterogeneous ones because brighter students stimulate remedial students toward more effective achievement and attitudes. The conflict over grouping of students goes back at least to 1923 (16:154-161) and does not appear to have progressed beyond the debating point.

Grouping by personality traits appears to be no more effective in determining student attitudes toward the achievement of remedial course objectives than grouping by intellect (145:43). One investigation found that students with similar personalities who were grouped together in remedial courses tended to have negative perceptions more frequently than those grouped by intellect (145:44). This finding has been attributed to personality clashes of "likes" which are more frequent and stronger than personality clashes of "opposites," because these conflicts involve more self-improvement along similar lines. The entire subject of homogeneous grouping is fraught with controversy.

SUMMARY

There is a paucity of research on the efficacy of remedial programs in the junior college. Indeed, with few exceptions, community colleges neither describe nor evaluate their endeavors in this critical area. Available research will not support the contention that junior colleges offer programs that in fact remedy student deficiencies. Programs are certainly offered, but the entire issue of remedying deficiencies has not been sufficiently researched to date.

Those few junior colleges that have evaluated the success of their remedial programs found that their programs were not remedying student deficiencies to a point where remedial students could enter regular college credit courses upon completion of the remedial course. In these institutions, student achievement and student persistence were not nearly sufficient to warrant continuation of a program designed to remedy deficiencies. Instead, the emphasis and focus were shifted to general education with another prime consideration being job placement following the program (108). The knowledge that the programs failed to remedy deficiencies is valuable for program modification, yet a more critical question involves the reasons the programs failed. Can student deficiencies be remedied? Can a junior college remedial course rightfully expect to accomplish in one or two semesters what the public schools have failed to accomplish

47

in twelve years? Answers to these and other related questions are not available; and the community junior college has based its remedial programs on unproved assumptions.

The behavioral sciences have contributed significant knowledge to the teaching process, most of which has not been incorporated into practice. For example, the matter of teacher attitudes has tremendous implications for junior college remedial programs. It has been suggested that if a teacher thinks that a given percentage of his students will fail, inevitably they will. On the other hand, if an instructor believes that students can succeed, student achievement is markedly increased (19).

Similarly, student attitudes are positively related to achievement and positive attitudes are generally associated with a minimum of student anxiety. Negative student attitudes can be minimized by insuring that teachers with positive attitudes (volunteers) are assigned to teach remedial courses. Research has also indicated that instructional techniques and processes are related to student achievement. Investigations in the behavioral sciences portend a need for increased experimentation and innovation in the teaching of remedial courses. Traditional approaches, such as the lecture method, do not appear efficacious in remedial courses. Experiments in courses with programed materials and audiovisual equipment have produced higher student achievement levels than have textbook-oriented courses.

Community colleges must seriously reconsider the practice of using only aptitude and achievement test scores for the purpose of placing students in remedial programs. The research indicates that these instruments have validity when used *in conjunction* with other predictors. Nonintellective factors appear to be positively related to student success and should be considered by junior colleges as an added factor in the placement of remedial students (54). One thing is clear: there appears to be little positive correlation between standardized test scores and student success in remedial courses. These instruments may be quite acceptable as sorting devices for regular college credit classes, but that they are adequate criteria in themselves for placing students in remedial programs is open to question. If test scores are going to be used for placement purposes, they should be used to determine student achievement in the remedial program as well as student readiness to enter regular college credit classes. No research is available to validate the practice of evaluating students on the basis of grades earned in remedial programs, because grades earned have not been demonstrated to be related to scores achieved on a given test.

The concept of homogeneous grouping needs further study before decisions are made in either direction. The available research on remedial programs is not particularly encouraging. Attrition rates in these programs are reaching alarming proportions. The knowledge that programs are not working well at present, coupled with some indications of techniques and approaches that appear sound, portend the need for new experiments in junior college remedial programs. Community junior college administrators are therefore encouraged to see what programs will work in their own institutions.

THE
IMPLICATIONS

chapter 8 Community colleges are and will continue to be "open-door" colleges. Historical precedent and state legislation have well established the concept of educational opportunity for all people. Community colleges are thus viewed as the means by which this lofty objective will be attained. It is obvious that as four-year institutions and universities raise entrance standards and tend to assume less and less responsibility for remedial programs, the junior colleges, with their open-door policies, are going to be forced to assume more and more responsibility. The open-door policy of admissions will be valid only if students are able to succeed in achieving their educational goals at the community college. It is to this end that community junior colleges must direct their attention if the door is truly to be "open," but not revolving. Perhaps it means that junior colleges must now determine what students are going to learn in remedial programs, the conditions of learning, and how this learning can be evaluated. This challenge is based on the premise that junior colleges should provide educational experiences for all students enrolled, and that student learning is a major institutional goal.

RESPONSIBILITY FOR STUDENT LEARNING It appears that no easy solution can be offered to the dilemma of the junior college and its ever increasing numbers of low-achieving students. Each institution is responsive to its sponsoring body—most typically, the community in which the two-year college is located. As long as boards of trustees do not raise embarrassing questions about the success or failure of students in remedial programs, there will be little pressure on administrators and instructors to evaluate their endeavors in remedial education. Yet, if two-year institutions accept responsibility for student learning, evaluation becomes essential to the remedial process, if for no other reason than that we know current institutional efforts at remediation are ineffective. It is suggested that junior colleges can no longer assume that programs "remedy" student deficiencies. Rather, it is obvious that two-year colleges are going to have to accept the challenge of student learning as the one criterion for success in any remedial program.

TEACHERS FOR REMEDIAL PROGRAMS

Research has shown that the inexperienced instructor is the one most often found in a remedial classroom (15:12). It is ironic that inexperienced teachers are sometimes considered to be unprepared to serve on major committees but yet are given one of the most difficult teaching assignments. The practice of assigning inexperienced teachers to teach remedial classes during their first year should be questioned unless they have received special training for remedial work.

Teacher attitudes are probably related to student achievement; accordingly, no teacher should be arbitrarily assigned to teach a remedial class who prefers not to do it or who is only mildly interested. It is unrealistic to expect uninterested teachers to motivate students who are characterized by their lack of motivation. Teachers must motivate students toward a desire to learn, and this may not be possible if teachers themselves are not enthusiastic.

The questions of status and prestige must be resolved if instructors are to become interested in the teaching of remedial students. Jargon is clouding the issues. If junior colleges are identified as institutions of higher education, then those who teach in two-year colleges are automatically associated with higher education. If the lives of students are important, all teaching assignments have value and worth. The pecking order of preferred teaching assignments is worthy of serious question and challenge.

Institutions may want to consider the possibility of employing qualified elementary teachers to teach students in remedial courses. Elementary teachers are experienced with the level of subject matter commonly taught in remedial courses. They are not subject matter specialists and the terms "college material" and "college level" may have little meaning or value to them when discussing a teaching assignment. One thing is quite clear: if subject matter specialists are not willing to instruct students enrolled in remedial courses, then other teachers must be found who will enthusiastically and competently provide instruction in the remedial programs. Remedial education is fast becoming the largest instructional endeavor of the two-year college, and instructors in these institutions can no longer avoid the issue. The problems are real and the students are real. Teachers are desperately needed.

Junior colleges would do well to develop in-service training programs on college time for faculty members to receive special training in the teaching and counseling of remedial students. Perhaps instructors in remedial programs must become specialists in learning if the community college is to implement the concept of the open door.

OBJECTIVES While educators universally agree that education serves as the medium through which culture is transmitted and through which individuals are socialized, there is no consensus on specific goals toward which remedial education programs are directed. Junior college administrators cannot agree on the tangible objectives of remedial education, much less on a program that would meet the objectives.

Instead of brandishing such generalities as "providing a second chance," "salvaging human resources" and "implementing the open door," junior college leaders and instructors must focus on specific instructional objectives (27:23), as follows:

1. Does the statement of objectives describe what the learner will be doing when he is demonstrating that he has reached the objective?

2. Does the statement of objectives describe the important conditions under which the learner will be expected to demonstrate his competence?

3. Does the statement of objectives indicate how the learner will be evaluated? Does it describe at least the lower limits of acceptable performance?

If community colleges are viewed only as some sort of "custodial" institution—to keep young people out of the employment market and off the streets—then new programs are urgently needed. Remedial education appears quite out of place in this context. A crucial issue is involved here, however. If junior colleges are assigned different functions at the institutional level, then programs must be devised and put into effect to properly fulfill these assigned tasks. It is unrealistic to think that any one program will adequately serve all of the functions identified with the junior college.

PROGRAMS IN REMEDIAL EDUCATION Available research shows little, if any, correlation between traditional programs and instructional processes and student learning. New approaches are needed. Methods and materials might deal with the subject matter to be taught in specific units of work which would be in agreement with realistic achievement levels for the students. Complex and abstract explanations could be avoided. Teachers might utilize materials which would enable the student, visually and verbally, to comprehend relationships between points. Methods and materials could be devised to take into account all of the student's linguistic deficiencies and limitations, as well as his interests.

Experimentation and innovation are desperately needed in the area of remedial education. The programs at Bakersfield College, Compton College, Contra Costa College, Los Angeles City College, and Forest Park Community College described in Chapter VI portend significant developments in program planning for remedial students. Many more such carefully designed programs are needed.

In addition to experimentation with certain variations in program planning and development, more experimentation is needed to determine the place and value of large-class and small-class instruction, team teaching, lay assistance, technological aid, and programed instruction—experimentation developed to facilitate individualized teaching so that each student's program could be designed with attention to what he already knows and needs to learn rather than accommodating the mythical remedial student. Junior college instructors and administrators need to explore more effective sources and programs if they are to justify the expenditures of time and money on a remedial teaching system which is proving to be ineffectual.

DIRECTIONS   Perhaps the best direction for improving remedial education is to investigate the areas of identification and description of the student requiring remediation as well as the evaluation of classes, curriculums, and programs designed for remediation. The area of identification and description is a basic requirement for any further effective direction. Evaluation is necessary for qualified statements of differences and of what is effective. How to identify a remedial student is generally not in question. Entrance scores in low percentile ranges and previous low academic achievement are usually considered sufficient information for identification.

This method of identification, however, does not automatically yield an adequate description of the student. Previous grades are of value, in addition to an overall general assessment, only to the extent that specific abilities can be listed as a result of knowledge of the grade. Knowledge of specific abilities, however, is usually not the information that grades provide. The information conveyed by a low grade is predominantly negative and suggests the abilities the student does not have. In the sense of not yielding information on a student's ability, scores in low percentile ranges are also negative when used to describe a remedial student. When a student performs poorly on a standardized test, it is likely that the test is too difficult. Tests too difficult or too easy do not provide good measurements.

An adequate description of the student is important for a well-specified curriculum and for planning curricular innovation. The more specific the description, the more it facilitates decision making and the formulation of fruitful hypotheses. The following suggestions are possible ways for improving the description of remedial students; they could also be incorporated in methods of identification.

1. Use a lower level test: After the identification of remedial students, those students could be retested with a lower level standardized test. For example, if a level I School and College Ability Test were used for initial testing, the remedial students could be retested with level II, a test designed for grades 10, 11, and 12. Other possible tests with lower levels for retesting might be the Cooperative English Tests, Cooperative Mathematics Tests, Sequential Tests of Educational Progress, and the California Tests of Mental Maturity. The latter, used with the California Achievement Tests, can provide an index to the degree a student is achieving above or below expectancy. Retesting at a lower level has the major advantage of providing scores that are more representative of students' abilities. These scores provide a more reliable profile for assessing differential abilities and a better baseline for measuring future achievement. Tests that are not too difficult for students also aid the actual testing situation by eliminating discouragement, excessive anxiety, and poor test-taking practices.

Information from retesting a remedial group would be useful for the following questions: (1) What is the range of ability in the remedial group? (2) For the purpose of grouping, to what extent can the remedial group be considered homogeneous? (3) What are realistic objectives for the remedial group? and, (4) What instructional materials are most consistent with the objectives and abilities of the remedial group?

2. Use different kinds of tests and instruments: To the extent that remedial students have difficulties related to factors other than achievement and ability, different kinds of descriptive information are valuable for curricular construction. Measurements from different kinds of tests, surveys, and inventories can aid in the prediction of college success, aid the counselor, and designate needed objectives. For example, results from remedial students on The Mooney Problem Check List: Form C could delineate the specific areas perceived by remedial students as problematic in college adjustment. Ten other possible problem areas are covered by the check list which contains 330 items, each representing a possible problem. How remedial students report their study habits and attitudes could easily have direct implication for the curriculum. An instrument designated to identify and aid in understanding students with academic difficulties is the Survey of Study Habits and Attitudes. Besides diagnostic usage, the survey can be used as a teaching aid for relaying effective study methods to the student.

Other kinds of measurements are provided by tests like the California Psychological Inventory which gives four categories of measures: (1) poise, ascendancy, and self-assurance; (2) socialization, maturity, and responsibility; (3) achievement potential and intellectual efficiency; and (4) intellectual and interest modes. Such scores could suggest assumptions on which to operate when selecting teachers, designating classroom procedures, and planning classroom environment. It might be found, for example, that the remedial group tends to be impatient with delay. Or members might be overly conforming, lacking in self-direction, rebellious toward rules, flexible, easygoing, defensive, etc.

Many tests of various kinds have potential value for describing remedial students and affording more rationale for planning remedial programs. Use of these tests can be maximized by a careful study of the tests, manuals, reviews, and bibliographies, and by referral of special questions and problems to the advisory services of test publishers. The number of statements derived from test results can be increased by testing students outside the remedial group for purposes of comparison. The feasibility of test administration, in terms of time, money, and personnel, can be improved by using random samples when the population of remedial students is large. Finally, the usefulness of different kinds of tests and instruments requires a reasonable attitude that seeks to employ the results effectively and avoids dismissal of the results because the accuracy of the measurement is not as great as one would like.

3. Improve communications with the remedial student: Status and associated roles, while adding structure and organization to social institutions and organizations, can inhibit communication. This fact suggests another possible fruitful area for obtaining descriptive information on remedial students. Students generally are not open with their criticisms of a teacher or teaching practice when in a situation that allows the teacher awareness of the criticism. In the presence of authority figures and peers, students are often inhibited because of embarrassment or fear of looking "stupid." .

The practice of eliciting anonymous answers to questions is one method of obtaining information on student problems and feelings. Valuable suggestions that might not otherwise be made can be obtained through anonymous answers. Answers to questions as simple as, "What do you like and dislike about this class?" or, "What would you like to see changed in this class?" can be examined and used to provide teacher and program evaluation. Other methods that improve communications through situations that avoid status influence and role expectancy can be designed to overcome student weariness in written expression and, also, designed to help the student learn to express himself better.

One method is to use opportunistically placed interviewers, perhaps students or personnel not identified with school staff. For example, during the time that students are adding and dropping classes, an interview could explore personal reasons for such changes. The popularity of sensitivity groups and the suggestion of Carl Rogers for basic-encounter groups in the school situation indicate another idea for improved communications. With a qualified person and an environment conducive to free expression, a variety of information and insights is possible.

After one critically investigates the best information and descriptions possible on the remedial student, a next step is to decide on changes for the remedial curriculum. These changes raise interest in their effectiveness and the question, "How do we know that these changes are producing the desired student changes?" Following are two evaluational techniques for answering such a question (49). To illustrate the techniques, an applicable situation is presented.

The remedial English teachers of a junior college have traditionally used instructional procedure "A." The goal of the remedial classes is to prepare students for a transfer English course. Descriptive information concerning the students suggests that they are not involved with English subject matter, and range in their abilities from a ninth to an eleventh grade level. The teachers note that approximately one-third of the students have poor attendance records and are not able to take sufficient class notes. With this and possibly more information, the teachers decide to try instructional procedure "B," which is a modification of "A" and has the objective of increasing English expression skills as measured by the English expression test of the Cooperative English Tests, a test for grades nine through twelve. For procedure "B" the teachers plan the following: (1) To use a series of programed materials designed to improve English expression and suitable for the ability range of the students. The programed materials are selected to minimize note taking and the effects of absenteeism. (2) To allow the students to select the materials with which they feel most secure. Student selection of materials is intended to start each student at an appropriate level and to promote student involvement in the materials.

Both mentioned techniques for evaluation have two common characteristics. First, both require two groups of students, a group that takes remedial English with procedure "A" and a group that takes remedial English with procedure "B." The other common characteristic is that both techniques require tests or measurements only at the end of the remedial classes. The first characteristic allows for the comparison of the two procedures within the institutional situation for which the change or innovation, procedure "B," was designed. The second characteristic allows for evaluation when initial test scores or measurements are not available.

TECHNIQUE I Technique I is not rigorous, and information derived by use of this technique should be handled with certain reservations. It has the advantage of practicality and usability when other techniques cannot be employed because of a lack of preparation. The technique can be summarized in four steps. First, select two groups from the remedial students. Second, use the two procedures. Third, test both groups at the same time. Fourth, compare the scores.

The groups selected might simply be two different classes. To the extent that the classes are the same—age of students, size of class, proportion of males and females, and proportion of students with special English problems (e.g., a foreign language background) —the final comparison, step four, tends to represent the actual difference in the effectiveness of "A" and "B" in increasing student test scores. Another similarity can exist between the classes if both had the same teacher. If the students who were in the class where procedure "A" was used score higher on the test, there is observable support to use the procedure in all remedial classes. A statistical treatment of the scores is valuable to demonstrate that the difference between the test scores of the two classes is not a difference that is so small that it would be expected simply by chance. Even if the difference in scores is statistically significant, the effectiveness of procedure "B" is open to question. The reason for this lack of certainty is that, when using technique I, there is no guarantee that the difference in test scores would not have occurred even if both groups had used procedure "A." To the extent that this is perceived as a possibility, the results of technique I should be used with reservation.

TECHNIQUE II

The second technique employs a more rigorous preparation, and results in statements that can be used with less reservation. Preparation involves the selection of the two groups through a method of random sampling. When the two groups for procedures "A" and "B" are randomly chosen, there is as good a guarantee as is generally possible that the two groups are initially equal on all the characteristics that will influence the final test scores. With this degree of guarantee there is less reason to believe that any final difference in test scores might have occurred even if procedure "A" had been used with both groups.

After group selection, the procedure for technique II is the same as for technique I. The groups are taught with the two procedures; both groups are tested at the same time, and the scores are compared. As with technique I, any method of equating the experiences for the two groups will improve the evaluation. The general logic for this evaluational technique is the following: If two groups are initially equal with regard to a given ability, and both groups have the same experiences with one exception; and if, after the experiences, the groups differ in regard to the given ability, then the difference can be accounted for by the exception.

Attempts to approximate the logical requirements in a school situation are difficult. The reward for the difficulty is greater confidence in one's effectiveness. The use of these and other techniques for evaluation has the expected result of providing the knowledge of what exceptions or changes produce the differences with remedial students.

A FINAL WORD

Clear definitions of intent and more imaginative procedures are necessary if community junior colleges are to implement the open door successfully. Traditional approaches simply are not doing an effective job of educating the low-achieving student.

BIBLIOGRAPHY

1. American Association of Junior Colleges. *Selected Papers* from the 47th Annual Convention, February 27-March 3, 1967, in San Francisco. Washington, D.C.: the Association, 1967.

2. Anderson, T. B. and Olsen, L. C. "Congruence of Self and Ideal Self and Occupational Choices." *Personnel & Guidance Journal* 44: 171-176; October 1965.

3. Andrews, Harlan F. *Project S.I.S.* A Preliminary Report. Sacramento, Calif.: Los Rios Junior College District, February 1966.

4. Atkinson, J. K. and Litwin, G. H. "Achievement Motive and Test Anxiety." *Journal of Abnormal Social Psychology* 60: 52-63; 1960.

5. Auburn University, School of Education. *Meeting Educational Needs for Post-High School Age Youth and Adults in Alabama* (A report of conferences held at Auburn University on Vocational, Technical, and Junior College Education.) Auburn, Ala.: Auburn University, 1964.

6. Basham, Garlyn A. "Legalized Loitering in California Junior Colleges." *Journal of Secondary Education* 36: 203; April 1961.

7. Bashaw, W. L. "The Effect of Community Junior Colleges on the Proportion of the Local Population Who Seek Higher Education." *The Journal of Educational Research* 58: 327-329; March 1965.

8. Becker, S. J. "Junior College Student." *Personnel and Guidance Journal* 44: 464-469; January 1966.

9. Berger, Emanuel. "Willingness To Accept Limitations and College Achievement: A Replication." *Journal of Counseling Psychology* 12: 176-178; 1965.

10. Blanton, F. L. *The Results of Two Experiments in Remedial Mathematics for College Freshmen at Abraham Baldwin College.* Research Report No. 64-2. Tifton, Georgia: Abraham Baldwin College Office of Institutional Research, January 1964. (Mimeo.)

11. Blocker, Clyde E.; Plummer, Robert H.; and Richardson, Richard C., Jr. *The Two-Year College: A Social Synthesis.* Englewood Cliffs, N.J.: Prentice-Hall, 1965.

12. Blocker, Clyde E. "Are Our Faculties Competent?" *Junior College Journal* 36: 12-17; December 1965.

13. Bogue, Jessie P. "Executive Secretary's Report." *Junior College Journal* 28: 482; May 1958.

14. Bossone, Richard M. "Understanding Junior College Students." *Journal of Higher Education* 36: 279-283; May 1965.

15. Bossone, Richard M. *Remedial English Instruction in California Public Junior Colleges: An Analysis and Evaluation of Current Practices.* Sacramento, California: California State De-

partment of Education, September 1966. (Mimeo.)

16. Burtt, H. E.; Chassel, L. M.; and Hatch, E. M. "Efficiency of Instruction in Unselected and Selected Sections of Elementary Psychology." *Journal of Educational Research* 14: 154-161; 1923.

17. California State Department of Education, Bureau of Junior College Education. *Student Majors by Curriculum Fields and Other Related Data in California Junior Colleges.* Sacramento, California: the Department, 1964.

18. Campbell, Doak S. "A Critical Study of the Stated Purposes of the Junior College." (Unpublished doctoral dissertation) Nashville: G. Peabody College for Teachers, 1930.

19. Canfield, Albert. "Two Years on the Road." (Speech) National Conference on the Experimental Junior College, Fourth Session. Los Angeles: University of California, July 11, 1967.

20. Casey, J. E. and Weaver, B. E. "An Evaluation of the Lecture Method and Small Group Method in Teaching in Terms of Knowledge of Content, Teacher Attitude and Social Status." *Colorado-Wyoming Journal of Academic Science* 4: 54; 1965.

21. Chamberlin, Robert. "A Plan of Course Appraisal and Curriculum Restriction for Barstow College, Aimed at Reducing Predictable Freshman Failures Related to Language Deficiency." (Seminar Paper) Los Angeles: University of California, School of Education, 1967. (Mimeo.)

22. Childers, Perry R. "A Two-Phase Analysis of the Summer on Trial Program at the University of Georgia." *The Personnel and Guidance Journal* 43: 929-933; May 1965.

23. Chrisman, Robert and Snyder, Hartland. *Application to the Danforth Foundation for Funds to Support the Contra Costa College Tutoring Program.* Contra Costa, Calif.: Contra Costa College, March 1966. (Mimeo.)

24. Clark, Burton R. "The 'Cooling Out' Function in Higher Education." *American Journal of Sociology* 65: 569-576; May 1960.

25. Clark, Burton R. *The Open Door College.* New York: McGraw-Hill Book Co., 1960.

26. Clarke, Johnnie R. "A Curriculum Design for Disadvantaged Community Junior College Students." (Unpublished doctoral dissertation) Gainesville, Fla.: University of Florida, 1966.

27. Cohen, Arthur M. "Developing Specialists in Learning." *Junior College Journal* 37: 21-23; September 1966.

28. Cohen, Arthur M. and Brawer, Florence B. *Focus on Learning: Preparing Teachers for the Two-Year College.* Occasional Report No. 11, Los Angeles: University of California, School of Education, Junior College Leadership Program, 1968.

29. Collins, Charles C. "Critical Problems of Students." *Junior College Journal* 36: 32-38; April 1966.

30. Contra Costa College, Research and Planning. *A Progress Report on Contra Costa College's Attempt To Improve Its Serv-*

ice to the Educationally Disadvantaged and/or Low-Ability Student. Contra Costa, Calif.: Contra Costa College, December 23, 1965. (Mimeo.)

31. Cooperative Research Monograph No. 3. *Research Problems in Mathematics Education.* Washington, D.C.: Government Printing Office, 1960.

32. Cosand, Joseph P. "Philosophy of Community Junior Colleges." *School and Community* 53: 35-36, 87-91; November 1966.

33. Dallas County Junior College District. *Experimentation at El Centro College:* the District, 1967. (Mimeo.)

34. D'Amico, Louis A. and Bokelman, Robert W. "Tuition and Fee Charges in Public Junior Colleges, 1961-1962." *Junior College Journal* 33: 36-39; September 1962.

35. D'Amico, Louis A. and Prahl, Marie R. "A Follow-Up of the Educational, Vocational and Activity Pursuits of Students Graduated from Flint Junior College, 1953-1956." *Junior College Journal* 29: 474-477; April 1965.

36. Davidoff, Foster. *The Opportunity To Succeed.* Compton, Calif.: Compton College, September 1967. (Mimeo.)

37. Davis, Allison. "Cultural Factors in Remediation." *Educational Horizons* 43: 231-251; 1965.

38. Davis, Elton C. *A Creative Methods Approach for Low Achieving Students.* Pasadena, Calif.: Pasadena City College, 1966. (Mimeo.)

39. Decker, R. D. "Out of Necessity: The Community College." *The Texas Outlook* 49: 36 and 50; January 1965.

40. DeHart, A. Robert. *The Junior College: An Open Door or a Revolving Door?* A paper presented at the 1962 American Personnel and Guidance Association Convention. Los Altos Hills, Calif.: Foothill College, 1962. (Mimeo.)

41. DeHart, A. Robert. *Tests for Screening and Course Placement.* A paper presented at the Conference of the American Association of Junior Colleges. Washington, D.C.: the Association, 1963.

42. Developmental Studies Workshop. *The Challenge for the Future.* Los Angeles: Los Angeles City College, June 3, 1967. (Mimeo.)

43. Di Vesta, F. J. "Instructor-Centered and Student-Centered Approaches in Teaching a Human Relations Course." *Journal of Applied Psychology* 38: 329-335; 1954.

44. Fields, Ralph R. *The Community College Movement.* New York: McGraw-Hill Book Co., 1962.

45. Florida State Department of Education. *The Community Junior College in Florida's Future.* Tallahassee: the Department, 1957.

46. Florida State Department of Education, State Junior College Advisory Board. *Five Years of Progress: Florida's Community Junior Colleges.* Tallahassee: the Department, 1963.

47. Florida State University and the University of Florida. *Improvement of Instruction*. Proceedings of the Fourth Junior College Administrative Teams Institute. Pensacola, Florida: July 27-31, 1964. (Mimeo.)
48. Fretwell, E. K., Jr. "Helps for Heresy Hunters." *Junior College Journal* 36: 16-19; November 1965.
49. Gage, N. L., editor. *Handbook of Research on Teaching*. Chicago: Rand McNally and Company, 1963.
50. Garrison, Roger H. "Reality and Illusion in Teaching." *Junior College Journal* 34: 15-19; February 1964.
51. Garrison, Roger H. "Leading the Collegiate Horses to Water." *Junior College Journal* 36: 26-28; November 1965.
52. Garrison, Roger H. "The Teacher's Professional Situation." *Junior College Journal* 37: 15-19; March 1967.
53. Garrison, Roger H. *Junior College Faculty: Issues and Problems*. Washington, D.C.: The American Association of Junior Colleges, 1967.
54. Gelso, Charles J. *Academic Adjustment and the Persistence of Students with Marginal Academic Potential Through Their Freshmen Year in College*. Douglas, Ga.: South Georgia College, June 1966. (Mimeo.)
55. Gibb, L. M. and Gibb, J. R. "The Effects of the Use of Participative Action Groups in a Course of General Psychology." *American Psychologist* 7: 247; 1952.
56. Gleazer, Edmund J., editor. *American Junior Colleges* 6th edition. Washington, D.C.: American Council on Education, 1963.
57. Gleazer, Edmund J. "The Rise of the Junior College from High School Extension to Higher Education." *College and University Business* 37: 64-67; October 1964.
58. Gleazer, Edmund J. "Junior Colleges Grow Up—Professionally." *College and University Business* 37: 62-64; November 1964.
59. Gleazer, Edmund J. "Junior Colleges Will Expand in Importance." *College and University Business* 37: 44-46; December 1964.
60. Gooder, Glenn G. *The Developmental Studies Workshop*. Los Angeles: Los Angeles City Junior College District, 1967. (Mimeo.)
61. Gregory, Merry A. "An Analysis of the College Preparation Developmental Program for Low-Achieving High School Graduates at Grand Rapids Junior College." (Unpublished doctoral dissertation) East Lansing, Mich.: Michigan State University, 1966.
62. Gunter, G. G. and McNitt, Helen. *Effectiveness of an Interest-Motivated Approach to Junior College Remedial English Instruction*. York, Pa.: York Junior College, 1966.
63. Hamilton, Robert S. and Heinkel, Otto A. *English A: An Evaluation of Programmed Instruction*. San Diego, Calif.: San Diego City Colleges, Curriculum Office, March 29, 1967.

64. Handy, Russell F. "An Analysis of Academic Improvement in the Basic Studies Program in Miami-Dade Junior College." (Unpublished doctoral dissertation) Miami, Fla.: University of Miami, 1965.

65. Harris, Norman C. *Curriculum Development for Hawaii's Community Colleges with Emphasis on Occupational Education.* Honolulu: Community College System of Hawaii, December 1964.

66. Havighurst, Robert J. and Rodgers, Robert. "The Role of Motivation." Chapter VII in Bryon S. Hollinshead *Who Should Go to College?* New York: Columbia University Press, 1952.

67. Havighurst, Robert J. "Social Change and the Community College." *North Central Association Quarterly* 41: 241-248; Winter 1967.

68. Hess, Robert D.; Shipman, Virginia; and Jackson, Darrel. "Some New Dimensions in Providing Equal Educational Opportunity." *Journal of Negro Education* 34: 220-231; 1965.

69. Hillway, Tyrus. *The American Two-Year College.* New York: Harper and Brothers, 1958.

70. Holmgren, Roy H. *Correlation Between English Ability and Success in Elementary Algebra.* San Mateo, Calif.: College of San Mateo, 1966.

71. Hopper, Harold H., and Keller, Helen. "Teaching Writing Skills in Large Classes." *Junior College Journal* 37: 41-43; November 1966.

72. Hoy, John C. "The Academic Procession Meets the Population Bulge." *Junior College Journal* 34: 25-27; February 1964.

73. Hoyt, Donald P. "Predicting Grades in Two-Year Terminal Programs." *Junior College Journal* 36: 20-24; February 1966.

74. Inlow, Gail M. "Factors That Influence Curriculum Change." *Educational Leadership* 23: 39-44; 1965.

75. Jefferson, Thomas. Letter to Colonel Charles Yancey, January 6, 1816.

76. Johnson, B. Lamar. *New Directions for Instruction in the Junior College.* Occasional Report No. 7, Los Angeles: University of California, School of Education, Junior College Leadership Program, March 1965.

77. Johnson, B. Lamar, editor. *Systems Approaches to Curriculum and Instruction in the Open-Door College.* Occasional Report No. 9, Los Angeles: University of California, School of Education, Junior College Leadership Program, 1967.

78. Johnson, Franklin R. "An Experimental Program for Students Scoring Below Regular Entry Level in Vocational Aptitude Tests at Los Angeles Trade-Technical College." (Seminar Paper) Los Angeles: University of California, School of Education, March 1967. (Mimeo.)

79. Kansas Legislative Council. Committee on Education. Advisory Committee on Junior Colleges. *Community Junior Colleges*

Summary Report: the Council, October 1964.

80. Kipps, Carol. "Arithmetic in College." *Junior College Journal* 37: 38-44; December 1966.

81. Kipps, Carol. "Basic Arithmetic Offered in California Public Junior Colleges." (Unpublished doctoral dissertation) Los Angeles: University of California, School of Education, 1966.

82. Kipps, Carol. "Progress Report on the First Semester of the Level I Program at Compton College." Compton, Calif.: Compton College, 1966. (Mimeo.)

83. Lombardi, John. "Faculty in the Administrative Process." *Junior College Journal* 37: 9-14; November 1966.

84. Lombardi, John. "The Challenge for the Future." (Speech given at the Developmental Studies Workshop, Los Angeles City College, June 3, 1967.) Los Angeles: Los Angeles City School Districts, June 3, 1967.

85. Lombardi, John. *The Experimental Junior College.* (Position Paper Prepared for Seminar on the Experimental Junior College) Palo Alto, Calif.: Science Research Associates, February 24, 1967. (Mimeo.)

86. Luke, Orral A. "A Study: Probation at Entrance." (Research Paper) Bakersfield, Calif.: Bakersfield College, June 1966. (Mimeo.)

87. Luke, Orral A. "A Ten Year Report of an Experimental Program for Low Ability Students." (Research Paper) Bakersfield, Calif.: Bakersfield College, June 1966. (Mimeo.)

88. Machetanz, Fred. *Evaluation of the Threshold Program at Los Angeles Valley College, Second Report.* Van Nuys, Calif.: Los Angeles Valley College, October 1966. (Mimeo.)

89. Martyn, Kenneth A. *Increasing Opportunities in Higher Education for Disadvantaged Students.* A report prepared for the Coordinating Council for Higher Education. Sacramento, Calif.: July 1966.

90. McKeachie, W. J. "Class Size and Class Influence." *Journal of Psychology* 45: 67-77; 1952.

91. Medsker, Leland L. *The Junior College: Progress and Prospect.* New York: McGraw-Hill Book Co., 1960.

92. Meister, M. "College Program for the Disadvantaged: College Discovery Program." *Science Education* 50: 406-408; December 1966.

93. Meister, M. and Tauber, A. "Experiments in Expanding Educational Opportunity for the Disadvantaged at Bronx Community College." *Phi Delta Kappan* 46: 340-342; March 1965.

94. Merson, Thomas B. "Let's Find the Answers." (Speech) American Personnel and Guidance Association, Denver Hilton Hotel, March 28, 1961. (Mimeo.)

95. Merson, Thomas B. "Teaching the Special Student: Developmental Programs." *Selected Papers* from the 47th Annual Convention, February 27-March 3, 1967, in San Francisco.

Washington, D.C.: American Association of Junior Colleges, 1967.

96. Metfessel, Newton S. "Student Characteristics of Under-Achieving and Low-Ability Students with Implications for Teaching Methods and Curriculum Planning." (Speech) Los Angeles: Los Angeles City College, Developmental Studies Workshop, September 13, 1966.

97. Michigan. The Department of Public Instruction. Committee on Post-Twelfth Grade Community Education. *Community College Instructional Program Development.* Bulletin No. 366. Lansing, Michigan: the Department, 1963. (Mimeo.)

98. Miley, Charles H. "They Leave for Many Reasons." (Research Paper) Fort Lauderdale, Fla.: Junior College of Broward County, no date. (Mimeo.)

99. Morrisett, Lloyd N. "Educational Assessment and the Junior College." *Junior College Journal* 37: 12-15; March 1967.

100. National Conference on the Teaching of English in the Junior College. *Research and the Development of English Programs in the Junior College.* Tempe, Arizona: Arizona State University, 1965.

101. National Council of Teachers of English. *Research and the Development of English Programs in the Junior College.* Proceedings of the Tempe Conference, 1965. Champaign, Illinois: the Council, 1965.

102. National Society for the Study of Education. *The Public Junior College.* The 55th Yearbook, Part I, Chicago: University of Chicago Press, 1956.

103. Nichols, Edith J. "Remedial Reading as a Function of the Junior College." (Seminar Paper) Los Angeles: University of California, School of Education, June 1967. (Mimeo.)

104. O'Connell, Alfred C. "The Open Door—A License to Fail?" *Junior College Journal* 31: 241; January 1961.

105. Parker, Franklin and Bailey, Ann. *The Junior and Community College, A Bibliography of Doctoral Dissertations,* 1916-1963. Washington, D.C.: American Association of Junior Colleges, 1965.

106. Peterson, Basil H. *Critical Problems and Needs of California Junior Colleges.* Modesto: California Junior College Association, Committee on Institutional Research, 1965.

107. Plummer, Robert H. and Richardson, Richard C. "Broadening the Spectrum of Higher Education." *Journal of Higher Education* 35: 308-312; June 1964.

108. Powell, Hope M. *Implementing a Curriculum for Provisional Students.* Los Angeles: Los Angeles City College, January 1966. (Mimeo.)

109. Prediger, Dale J. "Prediction of Persistence in College." *Journal of Counseling Psychology* 12: 62-67; 1965.

110. President's Commission on Higher Education. *Higher Educa-*

tion for American Democracy: Establishing the Goals. (A report of the President's Commission on Higher Education.) Washington, D.C.: Government Printing Office, December 1947.

111. President's Commission on Higher Education. *Higher Education for American Democracy.* New York: Harper and Brothers, 1948.

112. President's Commission on National Goals. *Goals for America.* Englewood Cliffs, N.J.: Prentice Hall, 1961.

113. Pyle, Gordon B. "Community Colleges and General Education in a Free Society." *Journal of General Education* 18: 227-238; January 1967.

114. Ravetch, Herbert. "A Critical Analysis of the Terminal English Course in the Junior College." (Seminar Paper) Los Angeles: University of California, School of Education, March 11, 1967. (Mimeo.)

115. Richards, J. M., Jr. "Description of Junior Colleges." *Journal of Educational Psychology* 57: 207-214; August 1966.

116. Richardson, Richard C., Jr. *Evaluation of the General Curriculum.* St. Louis, Mo.: Forest Park Community College, April 25, 1966. (Mimeo.)

117. Richardson, Richard C., Jr. and Elsner, Paul A. "General Education for the Disadvantaged." *Junior College Journal* 36: 18-21; December 1965.

118. Roman, Paul A. "A General Studies Program for Low-Achieving Students." (Seminar Paper) Los Angeles: University of California, School of Education, June 1966. (Mimeo.)

119. Roueche, John E. *The Junior and Community College, A Bibliography of Doctoral Dissertations, 1964-1966.* Washington, D.C.: American Association of Junior Colleges, 1967.

120. Roueche, John E. "Research Studies of the Junior College Dropout." *Junior College Research Review* 2: October 1967.

121. Roueche, John E. "The Junior College Remedial Program." *Junior College Research Review* 2: November 1967.

122. Saiko, Laura. "The Problems of Teaching in Community Colleges." *Journal of Higher Education* 35: 384-385; October 1964.

123. Scannell, William J. "What Do Teachers Think about English in the Two-Year College?" *Junior College Journal* 37: 24-29; September 1966.

124. Schenz, Robert F. "An Investigation of Junior College Courses and Curricula for Students with Low Ability." (Unpublished doctoral dissertation) Los Angeles: University of California, School of Education, 1963.

125. Schenz, Robert F. "What is Done for Low Ability Students?" *Junior College Journal* 34: 22-28; May 1964.

126. Seibel, Dean W. *Testing Practices and Problems in Junior Colleges—A Survey.* Field Studies Report—2. Princeton, N.J.:

Educational Testing Service, September 1966.

127. Selznick, Philip. "A Sociologist Views Junior College Admissions." *Journal of Secondary Education* 36: 33-38; January 1961.

128. Shea, John J. *Project PREP: A Program for Recovering and Extending Academic Potential for High School Underachievers Seeking Entrance at a Regional Community College.* Greenfield, Mass.: Greenfield Community College, June 1966. (Mimeo.)

129. Shepherd, Rod. "Guidelines and Practices in Curriculum for the Disadvantaged Junior College Student." (Seminar Paper) Los Angeles: University of California, School of Education, February 1967. (Mimeo.)

130. Smith, G. W. "Junior Colleges, Fish and Fowl." *Illinois Education* 52: 190-192; January 1964.

131. State Junior College Advisory Board. Task Force on the Junior College Student. *Florida's Community Junior Colleges; Their Contributions and Their Future.* Tallahassee: the Board, September 1962.

132. Stein, Ruth S. *Some Concepts Held by Los Angeles City College Entrants on Probation Because of Low SCAT Scores.* Los Angeles: Los Angeles City College, November 1966. (Mimeo.)

133. Stewart, L. H. "Characteristics of JC Students in Occupationally Oriented Curricula." *Journal of Counseling Psychology* 13: 46-52; Spring 1966.

134. Sugarman, Michael N. "What about the Dropouts?" *Michigan Education Journal* 44: 43; April 1967.

135. Swanson, Herbert L. "An Investigation of Institutional Research in the Junior Colleges of the United States." (Unpublished doctoral dissertation) Los Angeles: University of California, School of Education, 1965.

136. Thelen, Alice. *A Study of Academic Characteristics of General Curriculum Students after One Semester, One Year, in the General Curriculum Program.* St. Louis, Mo.: Forest Park Community College, September 12, 1966. (Mimeo.)

137. Thornton, James W., Jr. *The Community Junior College* (Second Edition). New York: John Wiley & Sons, 1966.

138. Topik, Ellida. *Predictions and Programs in Psychology Pertaining to the Ineffective College Student.* Los Angeles: East Los Angeles College, 1966. (Mimeo.)

139. Wattenbarger, James L. and Godwin, Winfred L., editors. *The Community College in the South: Progress and Prospects,* 1962. A report of the Southern States Work Conference, Committee on Education Beyond the High School, Sponsored by State Departments of Education and State Education Association.

140. Wattron, Frank. "A Proposed Course in the Popular Arts for Low Ability Junior College Students." (Seminar Paper) Los

Angeles: University of California, School of Education, May 1966. (Mimeo.)

141. Weber, C. "An Experimental Course in Remedial Writing." *Junior College Journal* 24: 285-286; January 1954.

142. Whitten, Betty. "Every Teacher a Spoilsport." *Junior College Journal* 36: 24-26; October 1965.

143. Young, Edwin A. *An Experimental Program for Low Ability Students.* (Second Progress Report) Los Angeles: Los Angeles City College, February 1966. (Mimeo.)

144. Yuhl, Walter A. "The Rationale, Structure and Evaluation of a Selected Terminal Social Science Program." (Seminar Paper) Los Angeles: University of California, School of Education, March 1967. (Mimeo.)

145. Zucker, Alfred. "An Investigation of Factors Contributing to and Interfering with the Successful Achievement of Remedial English Course Objectives in Los Angeles City Junior Colleges." (Unpublished doctoral dissertation) Los Angeles: University of California, School of Education, 1966.

146. Zucker, Alfred. "The Administrative Implications for the Junior Colleges of the New State Mandated Program for the Lowest Ten Percent of California's High School Graduates." (A post-doctoral research study) Los Angeles: University of California, School of Education, December 1966. (Mimeo.)

147. Zwicky, Laurie. "A Successful Intellectual Orientation Program." *Journal of College Student Personnel* 6: 200-202; June 1965.

DATE DUE
